Alice and Alfie
and the
magic windmill

BEST FRIENDS

written and illustrated by

Loykey & Lillybit

A CIP record of this book
is available from the British Library

ISBN 978-0-9562333-4-9

Alice and *Alfie* are on their final journey with more exciting adventures together with cheeky little Ted.
Continuing to keep the magic alive for all the children worldwide.

Twenty years later Nichole has grown into a fine young lady with a family of her own.

Nichole has one last wish that will surprise and delight *Alice*, *Alfie* and Ted, who remain Best Friends forever.

Join them on their magical journey, with their friend Mr. Moon shining from afar.

CONTENTS

Alice and *Alfie*
BEST FRIENDS

THE MAGIC WINDMILL WAKES UP........ 1

RAG AND BONES..................................... 15

THE MAGIC GARDEN COMES ALIVE..... 31

THE REMOTE CONTROL.......................... 47

THE VISIT... 61

A BIRTHDAY TREAT - BON APPETIT....... 75

THE TAKEAWAY...................................... 89

PENNIES FROM HEAVEN........................ 107

RETURN TO SENDER.............................. 123

CONTENTS

Alice and *Alfie*
BEST FRIENDS

SUITED AND BOOTED.............................. 141
BEE HIVE YOURSELF................................ 159
TIME WILL TELL...................................... 175
THE PUZZLE.. 195
A CHRISTMAS WISH COMES TRUE......... 107
HAPPY NEW YEAR.................................... 123
A STORY NEVER TO BE TOLD.................. 123
THE PRAM RACE...................................... 107
A MAGIC ENDING..................................... 123

Alice and *Alfie*

THE WINDMILL WAKES UP

Alice, *Alfie* and Ted's adventures had led them to the magic castle. They knew they had to leave the magic windmill because if Nichole took them back to England they would have all fallen asleep again.

It had been two weeks since they had left the windmill. The Wooden Prince was at home at the Castle just for Christmas. *Alice* and *Alfie* were so happy to see him, but Ted was not! The Wooden Prince kept looking at the bear, thinking he could put him in the cauldron of stew to 'Ted' it up a bit. Of course, the Prince was only joking.

Every night they would all sit round the big log fire sharing stories about their time away from each other. The Wooden Prince told them he would have to return to the Island in a couple of days but they were welcome to stay whenever they wanted.

Alice said to *Alfie*, "We should really go back to the windmill because if we stay away too long we might fall asleep here at the Castle and nobody would know that the windmill's magic keeps us awake."

Ted looked at *Alice* and *Alfie* and nodded his head then said, "Can we go back as soon as possible? We don't want the Wooden Prince to take us with him."

3

That night when they all went upstairs to bed they could see the Moon shining. *Alice* opened up the window and the Moon smiled and looked over towards the woods and told them, "Don't worry I will ask the wind to start blowing, which will help you get back to the windmill. Oh, and by the way, Nichole has already gone back home to England and Jacques has gone away, leaving the windmill sad and lonely. So, you see it is a good time for you all to leave."

Alfie suggested they could leave in the morning after they had eaten breakfast. The Moon laughed and said, "All of you are always thinking of your tummies."

"Of course," *Alfie* replied with a big grin.

The rag dolls went off to sleep apart from Ted. He sat up all night making sure they were not packed in a suitcase by the Wooden Prince.

Ted looked out of the window all night at the stars and the Moon. There was one bright star, Nichole's of course.

They woke up to a beautiful sunny day and all the snow had melted, leaving the grass so green. Ted muttered, "Old drip has gone, I bet."

Alice looked so sad knowing that Mr. Snowman would not be there.

4

Alfie whispered, "Don't worry, *Alice*, you know he will be back next year."

After breakfast it was time to say goodbye to the Wooden Prince. He gave them a key to the door of the magic castle and told them that they could come and stay at any time and use it as their home.

Alice, *Alfie* and Ted put on their rucksacks and picked up their skis but could not use them without the snow. They all hugged each other with tears in their eyes. Even Ted had one. Ted argued that it was a rain drop. *Alfie* said, "No it can't be the sun is shining."

They all walked towards the magic windmill, waving goodbye to the Wooden Prince. When they arrived at the woods they glanced back, and the magic castle had disappeared.

As they walked through the woods they could hear all the sounds of the animals and birds. *Alfie* asked *Alice*, "I wonder why Jacques has gone away?"

She replied, "Holiday time for him again, he does work so hard."

When they arrived at the sty next to the river *Alfie* shouted, "Look, what luck. The boat from the magic windmill." It was as if it had come to take them home.

Alice, Alfie and Ted jumped on board and hoisted up the sail and off she went.

Finally, they reached the bridge. Alfie pulled down the sail, so the boat could go under. Alice shouted, "Everybody duck."

Ted was fast asleep and was woken and as he jumped up he turned and the top of the bridge hit him on the head, knocking him off the boat. He fell with a big splash and Alice and Alfie just laughed. He managed to pull himself up on the river bank, but the boat kept on going. Alice shouted, "See you back at the windmill and it will give you time to dry off."

In the distance Alice and Alfie could see the magic windmill with the sails turning so fast. Alfie said to Alice, "Are you sure Jacques is not there? Perhaps he is working, as the sails are going around."

Alice replied, "No it's only the wind, I am sure; the Moon told us Jacques was away."

The boat eventually stopped at the jetty outside the windmill. Alice and Alfie jumped off. They both shouted at the same time. "It's good to be back."

They walked round to the front door, *Alfie* tried to open it but it was locked. So he ran around to the ladder at the side of the windmill and up he went followed by *Alice*. They sat on the windowsill and spotted Ted walking back, moaning to himself, so *Alice* went downstairs to open the back door for Ted as there was no way he would make it up the ladder.

Alfie walked into the kitchen and was knocked over by the mice. "Slow down," he shouted.

The mice told them that Jacques had been taken to the Hospital. He had not been very well.

Just then Ted walked in and said, "Thank you, for not waiting for me! I am full of tadpoles and croaking like a frog." *Alice* told him to sit down and she would light the fire. As she turned, she saw a letter from Nichole.

> *Dear Alice, Alfie and Ted*
> *As you are reading this letter I know*
> *you are back, and I understand why*
> *you left. It was for the best.*
> *Look after yourselves and always*
> *be best friends. The windmill will keep*
> *you safe. Hopefully see you in May so*
> *pray for that day.   Love Nichole xxx*

Alice sat at the table with tears in her eyes. Ted was still moaning and as he looked across the kitchen he could see the cupboard door open. There was a big jar of honey. He just rubbed his tummy. *Alice* looked in the cupboard but there was not a lot else, so they decided to go to the village to see what they could find. Ted suggested he stay behind and look after the jar of honey. *Alice* nodded, "O.K., but I am going to mark the jar and the lid stays on until we come home." It drove him mad and made him sad.

Alice and *Alfie* returned after two hours to find Ted fast asleep in the bed box. *Alice* had found some bread and rolls at the Bakery and *Alfie* had a stroke of luck in the Butchers when somebody had left their bag of goodies and walked off. Outside he opened the bag to find a vegetable pie, eggs and fish.

Alice checked the jar of honey and was amazed that Ted had not touched a drop. She opened the honey, cut some bread and popped it on the table.

Ted thought he was dreaming and started sniffing in his sleep. It was so funny. He suddenly snored and woke himself up. "Great, let's all eat." He shouted.

That night *Alice* and *Alfie* spoke to the Moon and wished Jacques a speedy recovery. The Moon was glad to have them back. *Alice* blew him a kiss.

Alfie, the windmill will make Jacques better!

Alice and *Alfie*

RAG AND BONES

15

The next morning *Alice*, *Alfie* and Ted were all woken up by a big commotion downstairs. *Alice* opened the bedroom door very slowly. She could hear two voices downstairs; one of them was Kimmy, Jacques' friend. Then she heard the back door shut.

Alice, *Alfie* and Ted jumped up onto the window seat to have a look outside. Kimmy and another lady were waving to somebody down the lane, then up trotted an old horse and cart with a little old man shouting, "Rag and bones." Ted said, "He is definitely dressed in rags." *Alice* suggested they go downstairs to see what was going on.

Ted muttered, "I'm going back to sleep. The shouting has given me a big headache, and anyway I don't want to hear about the bones." *Alfie* opened the back door and looked out. In the porch were a load of old blankets and sheets. *Alfie* shouted to *Alice*, "Quick they are coming." *Alice* lifted the sheets and grabbed *Alfie* and they hid underneath them.

Kimmy walked in and told the rag man that there were some old rags and sheets that they had found while clearing out, as Jacques needed to buy some new ones.

Alice and *Alfie* were still underneath the sheets. The rag man picked up the rags and threw them in the cart.

Alfie popped his head up and *Alice* asked him "Can you see any bones?" *Alfie* replied, "No."

The horse and cart started to move, and the old man started shouting, "Rag and bones." Ted looked out of the window wishing he would stop. As the old man left the yard, Ted saw *Alice* and *Alfie* on the back of his cart, waving. *Alice* looked at *Alfie* and at the same time said, "This could be a new adventure, without Ted."

The old cart was wobbling from side to side and they were being thrown all over the place. They just laid in the sheets looking up at the sky. It was very cold with the wind blowing, so they cuddled up and fell asleep.

Meanwhile, back at the windmill, Ted was in his element. Kimmy and her friend had gone and lit the log fire and left a cupboard full of food. There was a note on the kitchen table welcoming Jacques back home.

Ted got stuck into the food and wondered to himself when *Alfie* and *Alice* would be back. Ted fell asleep next to the log fire and did not hear the kitchen door open. It was Jacques, wearing a plaster cast on his leg. The taxi driver put his bags down and Jacques thanked him for his help.

Just as Jacques went to stoke the fire he tripped and fell over Ted. He picked him up and looked right into his eyes. Ted had honey all round his mouth. Jacques thought how could that BEE! He took Ted over to the sink and washed his face, thinking that Kimmy had played a joke on him. He put Ted into the bed box and decided to sleep downstairs, as the stairs would be too much with his leg in plaster.

Meanwhile *Alice* and *Alfie* had woken up. The old cart was not moving. They found themselves in an old barn. The horse was feeding on hay over in the corner, but no sign of the rag man. The barn was stacked high with furniture, clothes and toys. *Alfie* ran over to the door, only to find it was locked. He shouted to *Alice*, "I think we are here for the night - I cannot see a way out."

The next morning back at the windmill Kimmy had turned up to make sure Jacques was o.k. and that he had had a good night's sleep. Jacques said that he was missing his old patchwork quilt. "It is very old, and my Mum made it for me." Kimmy told him that the rag and bone man was at the windmill yesterday and she had given him some old blankets and sheets; it must have been with them. "Sorry, Jacques." Jacques also told her that *Alice* and *Alfie* were missing, unless they were upstairs.

21

Kimmy went up to look and returned and told Jacques they were not up there. Jacques was in his rocking chair, laughing. Kimmy asked, "What is so funny?"

Jacques replied, "It was brilliant making me think that Ted had eaten all the honey by putting some round his mouth."

Kimmy told him, "You must have been dreaming!"

Ted slid down into the bed box. Jacques rubbed his eyes and whispered to Kimmy, "Did you see that?"

Kimmy replied, "You must be seeing things! Let us go and see if we can find your mother's quilt."

They went outside to the old van and helped him into the front. Ted suddenly ran outside and jumped into the driver's seat without them seeing him. Kimmy jumped in and sat on Ted. "Now, Jacques I know he is a good old Ted but why are we taking him with us?"

Jacques picked up Ted and put him in the windscreen, muttering to himself that was the windmill playing games.

Jacques asked Kimmy where the rag and bone man's yard was. She replied, "At the back of the railway station, unless he has moved."

Back at the barn the horse had been fed and the old cart was out in the yard ready for another day's work.

Alice and *Alfie* were still asleep under the old sheets as they had been up all night playing with the toys.

The rag and bone man had tripped over all the toys that the rag dolls had left everywhere. He fell so badly he had cracked a bone in his ankle. He had to lock up the yard and go to the hospital.

After a while he returned with a plaster cast on his foot. When Jacques turned up they were a matching pair. Mr Rag told Jacques that it was the toys that caused his accident. "Anyway, how can I help you?"

Kimmy explained what had happed to the quilt. Mr. Rag asked, "Would you like some lunch and after we can look for your quilt."

Kimmy explained she had shopping to do but Jacques could stay and she would pick him up later.

After lunch, Jacques and Mr. Rag sat out in the rocking chairs and dropped off to sleep.

Alice and *Alfie* had woken by Ted playing a penny whistle, badly. *Alice* grabbed Ted and the whistle then walked outside, only to see Jacques and Mr. Rag both in plaster. It was so funny!

25

Ted muttered, "When I broke my leg all by brothers and sisters wrote their names and funny sayings on my plaster cast."

Alfie scratched his head and suddenly remembered that there were some coloured pens in the barn. He ran in and picked up the pens. They all had one each and they crept over to Jacques and Mr. Rag. They had stopped rocking, and both had their legs up on stools.

Alice wrote on Jacques plaster cast:

'Looking cool, looking swell,
Hoping soon that you will be well
Love *Alice*'

Ted just put an X

Alfie took his bright red pen and wrote on Mr. Rag's plaster cast:

'Sorry, it was the rag dolls that broke your bones
And not the toys and the gnomes
From *Alfie*'

Jacques and Mr. Rag woke up just as Kimmy drove into the yard. She looked at them and said, "I see you have been writing on your plaster casts."

27

They both looked at each other, not knowing what to say. Jacques had some idea! Kimmy went into the barn and there on top of the pile of rags, was the old patchwork quilt.

Kimmy picked up the quilt and popped it straight in the van. There in the front window was *Alice, Alfie* and Ted. She scratched her head and thought it was very weird, what was going on.

Jacques and Mr. Rag said goodbye and would probably meet at the hospital when their casts were taken off.

Jacques squeezed into the front of the van and said, "Look! *Alice, Alfie* and Ted, where did you find them Kimmy?"

She replied, "Not me, it must have been you!"

Jacques replied, "Rag dolls don't have bones you know, so it must be the magic of the windmill."

When they arrived home, Kimmy put the rag dolls and Ted to bed.

It had got dark and *Alice* and *Alfie* looked at the Moon shining so bright and wished that Mr. Rag's bones would mend soon.

29

Alice said," Thank goodness we saw no bones."

Alice and *Alfie*

THE MAGIC GARDEN COMES ALIVE

Ted was up early which made a change. "It's Spring." He shouted. This woke *Alfie* up and he nudged *Alice*, "Ted is saying it is Spring." *Alfie* looked at him, half asleep and asked how he knew.

Ted said, "Look out of the window the daffolils have opened and the sun has a big smile on his face."

Alice and *Alfie* looked out of the window and there they were. They had been hidden away for nearly a year and now were showing their heads without any fear of Mr. Frost and the white fluffy snow.

Jacques was downstairs with his foot up thinking it was only five weeks to go until he could have the cast off his leg.

Alice and *Alfie* decided to go and see the daffodils, so they climbed down the ladder at the side of the window. There in front of them were heads of yellow gently blowing from side to side in the wind.

Alfie said, "Shall we pick some?" The daffodils all bowed their heads as if to say no. He resisted, deciding they would look just fine where they were.
Alfie was excited and said, "Do you know what this means, the Magic Garden is open."

They climbed back up the ladder. *Alfie* opened the bedroom door and they could hear Jacques snoring downstairs in front of the log fire. They crept downstairs followed by Ted.

Alice pulled the curtain open and there was the door to the magic garden with a sign saying, 'Open for Spring, eat all you like and don't pay anything.

Ted licked his lips and *Alice* said the magic words, "Dora Dora open so we can go and explora." The mice applauded her as she had remembered the magic words. The door opened and they all went out into the garden.

Spring had arrived, and the garden had come alive. *Alice* and *Alfie* sat down on the old bench and watched the animals having fun. Ted was filling his face with Spring honey and eventually had a very sore tum. *Alice* said, "I wish Nichole was here to see the magic garden now it has come alive."

Ted shouted, "We could make a lot of money you know, because every time I pick something it grows back instantly. We could sell the fruit and veg at the top of the lane on the old barrow which is in the barn. We could use the baskets for the fruit and veg, so all we have to find is an old pot to collect the money."

Alfie said, "What a brilliant idea and all the money could be donated to a charity. What about the hospital that has been caring for Jacques and Mr. Rag?" They all agreed and went back through the door of the magic garden.

Jacques was awake and had gone down to the riverbank to sit in the midday sun. *Alice* and *Alfie* ran across to the barn, closely followed by Ted, and there in the corner was the old barrow and the wicker baskets.

They pushed the barrow up to the top of the lane and then walked back to the magic windmill carrying the baskets. They went into the magic garden and filled the baskets with fruit and vegetables.

Alice fetched a paper and pen and wrote some labels with all the prices on. All they needed now was a pot. Ted said, "I have seen an old pot under the sink in the kitchen." It was an old chamber pot. None of them knew what it was for, but it would be perfect for collecting the money.

They all walked up to the end of the lane and put their baskets onto the old barrow. *Alice* put the labels out and the pot in the middle of the barrow between the baskets. They all hid behind the hedge.

After about thirty minutes Ted was fed up and muttered, "Waste of time. I am going back home for a nap." He wandered off down the lane and out of sight.

Suddenly a car pulled up and a little old lady got out. She walked over and picked up some carrots, potatoes, parsnips and asparagus. Then the sound they had been waiting for - clink, clink - the sound of the money being dropped into the potty. The car door shut and off she drove.

Alice and *Alfie* jumped up and there in the pot was a handful of euros. Once again, they decided to hide behind the hedge. Within minutes a man walking his dog stopped and yes, again, they hear the coins falling into the pot. This went on all afternoon until all the fruit and veg had been sold.

Alice and *Alfie* hid the cart behind the hedge and walked back to the magic windmill with empty baskets and a pot full of money. Every day was the same and by the end of the week the pot was full. So, *Alfie* decided to make a windmill money box and *Alice* painted it. Once it was dry they filled it with all the coins.

Alice and *Alfie* were worn out and went back to the windmill, climbed into their bed box and fell asleep.

Jacques had returned for lunch and he was making his sandwich when there was a knock at the door. He opened the door and there stood a little old lady. She said hello to Jacques and enquired if there was any more asparagus left as she should have bought more earlier that morning.

Jacques said, "I don't understand, but I do have some on the kitchen table, please take some." She left some money on the table, but Jacques said, "No I don't want any money." The lady told Jacques to put it in the charity box and left, happy with her asparagus, but a very confused Jacques.

The next day *Alice* and *Alfie* emptied the money box and when they counted the coins they had 250 euros. That night they put the money into an old sack with a note, from Jacques, *Alice* and *Alfie*, saying: "Thank you for my plaster cast and looking after me in the past."

Alice and *Alfie* decided to set off for the hospital as it was a long way. They eventually arrived and at the main door was a thermometer which was made of wood, with a big red stripe in the middle which indicated how much money had been raised.

Alfie said to *Alice*, "Look, they only need another 250 euros! What luck."

41

A lady opened the hospital door and *Alfie* left the bag of money at the base of the thermometer. As *Alice* coughed the old lady saw the sack laying on the floor. She opened it and her eyes lit up. She went back inside and *Alice* and *Alfie* set off home.

The next morning there was a knock at the door. When Jacques opened the door, there stood the doctor from the hospital. Jacques was surprised to see him and asked, "Hello, have you come to take the plaster off my foot?"

The doctor replied, "No, I have come to thank you for donating the money from selling fruit and vegetables from your magic windmill. The note inside said it was from Jacques, *Alice* and *Alfie*."

Jacques smiled and said, "It is a pleasure and I will donate again once my plaster cast is off."

As the Doctor was leaving he told Jacques he would take his plaster cast off next week and told him to bring *Alice* and *Alfie* with him.

When the Doctor had gone Jacques looked for *Alice* and *Alfie*, but they were nowhere to be seen; there was only Ted fast asleep in the bed box. Jacques knew it was *Alice* and *Alfie* up to their old tricks.

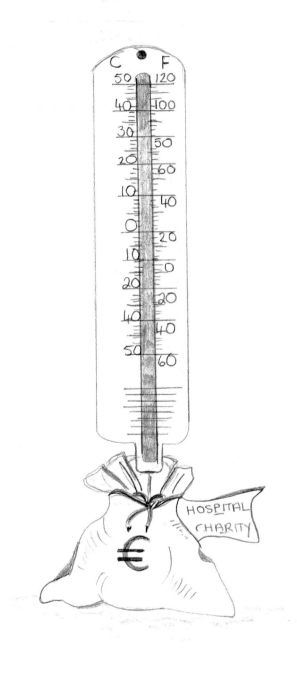

43

The next morning Jacques came back into the windmill after feeding the ducks and bumped into *Alice* and *Alfie*, knocking them to the floor. He picked them up and said, "Well, you two, I hope you don't mind hospitals, as next week you are coming with me to have my plaster cast off. How on earth did you make all the money? It must be all to do with the magic windmill."

Jacques put them back into the bed box next to Ted.

"*Alfie*, let us write on Jacques' cast again!"

Alice and *Alfie*

THE REMOTE CONTROL

Spring had really sprung with the birds nesting in the bird boxes. *Alfie* kept on opening the bedroom window and telling the swallows, "No, no, no, not on the windmill sails or you will lose your nest and your tails."

Jacques had worked out how the fruit and veg had been sold when Kimmy said she had seen the old cart at the end of the lane behind the bushes.

Early that morning there was a sound of a vehicle outside in the yard. *Alice* and *Alfie* looked out of the window and there was an old French van, with ladders tied onto the roof. The van had a sign which said, 'Aerial Man.'

Just then Ted looked over *Alfie's* shoulder, lifted his glasses and said, "What is going on?"

Alice replied, "It's an aerial man, whatever he is."

Then, a tall skinny man got out of the van and Jacques walked across to see him. They both started pointing up at the windmill, but *Alice* and *Alfie* could not hear what they were talking about.

Jacques came back inside, and the man slid two sets of ladders off the roof and lent them up against the windmill.

Alfie said to *Alice*, "There must be something wrong with the windmill I hope it is not sad news."

The aerial man opened the back doors of the van and took out a big wooden reel of black cable and climbed the ladder to the top of the roof.

Ted whispered, "Perhaps it's a new washing line. We need one, as the old one keeps breaking, especially when I'm swinging on it."

As the cable came up past their window Ted put out his paw and touched it. He said, "It's very shiny and slippery, not something that you would put washing on."

The man started to bang in clips that held the cable to the windmill. As he reached the bottom of the ladder, Jacques was coming out of the kitchen and said to the aerial man, "I have made some coffee! It is in the kitchen."

Alfie went out of the window and climbed onto the man's ladder.
Alice shouted, "Careful *Alfie*, one step at a time."

50

51

Eventually he reached the top of the ladder, it was a long way up.

Alice asked him, "What can you see?"

Alfie shouted down, "One way I can see the magic castle, and the other the church in the village."

Alice replied, "No, tell me what the cable is doing!"

Suddenly, the back door opened, and the man took out a metal contraption which looked like a flying saucer.

Alfie saw the aerial man at the bottom of the ladder and decided that it was no good, he had to jump. He landed on the sails of the windmill. *Alice* just gasped.
As the man walked up the ladder *Alice* sat still. The man saw her and whispered, "There will soon be a signal, you know."

Ted said, "What does that mean, a signal?"

Alice replied, "I have no idea." She glanced up and saw *Alfie* still hanging onto the sail.

The aerial man fitted the metal dish to the top of the windmill; then he clipped the black cable on. It looked like a big plate waiting for food. Then he tilted the dish towards the sun.

The aerial man pulled his ladders down and put them back on to the roof of the van.

Alfie could not hold on any longer and slid down the sail. As he came flying past the window, *Alice* reached out and caught hold of his leg and landed on the bedroom floor.

Alfie said, "That was lucky."

They all sat on the bed listening to Jacques talking to the aerial man. Then there was a loud noise of people talking, and music playing, but it was not them. The rag dolls could not make out what was going on. Then there was silence. All they could hear was Jacques thanking the aerial man for the set.

Ted said, "What is a set?"

Alfie shrugged his shoulders and replied, "Perhaps a new set of plates."

Alice laughed, "Plates don't play music or talk, do they?"

All evening they heard weird noises but could not go down to see what they were. At 10.30 there was silence and Jacques had obviously gone to bed.

The rag dolls crept downstairs; the log fire was still burning but no sounds of music or people.

Alfie said, "Look over in the corner, a black screen, what is that?"

Alice walked over and touched it and said to *Alfie* and Ted, "It is like glass." There was a black cable coming down the wall which went into the back of the glass panel.

Alfie muttered, "Well, we have a plate on the roof and a glass panel in the lounge, what is that all about?"

Ted had a glass of milk and sat down on the old sofa. As he moved his arm the black glass came alive. There were people moving and talking. *Alice* and *Alfie* ran and hid behind the sofa. *Alice* shouted, "What is it?"

Then Ted moved his bottom and the screen started playing music. Every time Ted moved it changed. Ted jumped up and it went blank, not a thing. As he sat down it started playing again. *Alice* realised it was something to do with the chair.

Next to Ted was a thin black object with lots of numbers and an 'Off' and 'On' switch.

Alice went over and picked it up and suddenly the glass screen came alive.

All night long they sat there playing with the control and watching the programmes.

The next morning Jacques got up early and as he walked into the lounge the Television was still on. *Alice*, *Alfie* and Ted were fast asleep in their bed box, with the remote control in Ted's paw. Jacques gently removed it from his clasp and turned it off.

Every night was the same and Jacques could not understand what was going on.

One night the moon shone down and said to *Alice* and *Alfie*, "I see you have found the remote control which brings the television alive from the sky above."

"Nichole also sends her love."

Alfie said, "That was the dish of the day."

Alice and *Alfie*

THE VISIT

Alice and *Alfie* could not wait for the evening to come, knowing that when Jacques went to bed that they could switch the magic screen on.

As they laid on the windowsill in the bedroom the phone rang. *Alice* listened at the top of the stairs and heard Jacques say, "Yes, yes, yes." But what was he saying yes to? Then he put the phone down.

Alfie asked *Alice* who it was. "I don't know, only that he said yes to somebody." she replied.

That evening when Jacques went to bed *Alice*, *Alfie* and Ted sat in front of the log fire and switched on the T.V. They ended up watching the shopping channel.
It was so funny, as Ted wanted to buy everything.

The next morning Jacques had to pick them all up and put them back into their bed box. He whispered to them, "Today is going to be a very noisy day, as children are coming to play."

Alfie only heard that children were coming to play.

He told *Alice* as she woke up. *Alice* asked, "What children?"

Alfie replied, "I don't know. Perhaps Nichole and Cleo are coming with their children."

Alice smiled and agreed, "Yes that must be it, as Nichole said that she would be back for a holiday."

The windmill started to shudder and, as they ran outside, they could see the sails beginning to move with the wind blowing them.

They could see Jacques in the windmill for the first time in a while. He was whistling while he was working. He seemed to be so happy,

Alice said, "Perhaps he was saying yes to the baker saying that he would grind some grain to make flour.".

Ted had gone off for a very long walk as he was so fed up with all the noise, while *Alice* and *Alfie* walked down to the bridge. The fish were having fun and *Alfie* said, "Shall I go and get the fishing rods?"

Alice replied, "No, how would you like to be caught on a hook and line?"

Just at that moment there was a hoot, hoot but it was not Mr. Owl. It was the old school bus; it had stopped in the yard at the windmill.

Alice and *Alfie* ran back to the windmill to see what was going on. They popped their heads around the corner of the windmill and they saw the door open. Thirty-eight children followed each other off the bus.

They all stood in the yard with their teacher as Jacques came out of the mill. He said to the teacher, "Hello I am glad you could all come. Now I can show the children how flour is made. They can all make some and take a bag home."

As the children walked into the mill *Alice* heard one little girl tell another, "This is where the rag dolls live. I am going to try and find them."

Alice whispered to *Alfie*, "Did you hear what that little girl was saying? She was the one from the school trip that we went on. She was not very nice to us!"

Alfie answered, "Yes I do remember. Let's play a game on her and her friend." So, *Alice* and *Alfie* climbed up the ladder and into the windmill and sat at the window.

The school teacher and children were all in the mill watching Jacques making the flour and the two little girls had gone off to look for the rag dolls.

The two little girls walked around the corner of the windmill. *Alice* tapped on the glass and the two little girls looked up, *Alice* waved. They both stood there rubbing their eyes and could not believe what they were seeing." Rag dolls can't wave, it must be the sunlight." They both agreed.

The sails were turning very fast and the girls went to the back door and went inside. They went through the kitchen and up the stairs. *Alice* and *Alfie* heard them coming so they opened the window and quickly climbed down the ladder. By the time the girls had reached the window, *Alice* and *Alfie* had run down to the river.

The girls looked out of the window and could see *Alice* and *Alfie* waving. They saw the ladder at the side of the window and decided to climb down. They took very small steps, but their scarves were blowing in the wind and caught on the sails which spun them round.

Alice and *Alfie* just laughed as they were spinning round. The little girls were screaming to stop the windmill and help them down.

Jacques and the teacher came running out to see what the noise was, followed by the children. They all just laughed, but the teacher was not amused.

Jacques, said, "I will try and stop the windmill sails, but it may take some time as the wind is very strong."

Jacques put the brake on but still this did not make a lot of difference.

Alice whispered to the wind, "Please stop as I think the little girls have now learnt a lesson." The wind heard and stopped blowing, but the little girls were stuck at the top of the windmill.

As this was all happening Ted walked back and just scratched his head and thought to himself, "Goodness me, Nichole has a lot of children now."

Alfie told him they were on a school trip from the local school.

Alice looked up and asked the wind, "Please can you blow very gently?" So, he did and down they came.

They were both told off by the teacher and the little girls blamed the rag dolls. The teacher said, "You two are always dreaming."

Before the children got back on the bus Jacques gave them all a bag of flour to take home for their Mums to bake with, except the two little girls who had been so naughty. They just went home with a good telling off.

The windmill stropped working, and Jacques was worn out and so was *Alice* and *Alfie*. It was all fun and games that day at the magic windmill, and the wind had fun as well.

That night the moon shone down and said that he had had fun watching. "Remember *Alice*, *Alfie* and Ted, when you upset somebody you could end up on your head."

73

Alfie said, "I don't know, KIDS."

Alice and *Alfie*

A BIRTHDAY TREAT - BON APPATITE

Summer was well on its way as the air was getting warmer, and the lavender had popped their heads out and the bees were having a feast on the nectar while Jacques was picking some lavender for the kitchen table.

Ted was in the rocking chair, but he was so small and light it would not rock; even the mice were laughing. Ted was reading a magazine that Jacques had left on the chair. He was looking at the front page when, suddenly, he shouted out, "It's my birthday."

Alice asked, "Do you have a birthday?"

"Yes, I can remember the day I was born." Ted said.

Alfie joked, "What factory was it?"

Ted replied, "I don't know but on my leg is a name tag." *Alice* lifted his trouser leg and sure enough there was a name tag. It said Made in England by Loykey & Lillybit with its own CE label.

Alfie just laughed and asked, "What sort of name is that, it sounds Chinese if you ask me." It had the date on, 2nd May, and *Alice* said, "Yes today is your birthday. What would you like to do as it's special?"

Alfie muttered, "Let him go and find a teddy bear's birthday party somewhere, then we can have a peaceful day."

Ted said, "It's my birthday, it's my birthday."

"He is going to be saying that all day," groaned *Alfie*.

Ted just sat there in the rocking chair looking at the magazine; then he shouted, "Look, the Zoo."

Alice and *Alfie* came over and it read, 'Come to the Zoo today, and bring your best friends with you.
Rag dolls, toys and teddy bears are all in for a treat.'

The zoo was a long way from the windmill. *Alice* said, "We shall go - it is Ted's birthday treat."

They packed a bag of goodies including honey for Ted's tummy. They all set off and when they reached the top of the lane Ted said, "My legs hurt,"

"What already," *Alfie* mumbled.

At the gateway was the old cart. There was no food on it, so *Alice* picked up Ted and put him on the cart. *Alice* asked, "Come on *Alfie*, help me push the cart."
"No, let's pull, it's much easier," *Alfie* suggested.

Off the rag dolls went, down through the woods. Ted shouted, "It's a bit bumpy you know."

Alfie told him, "You will have a bump on your head in a minute if you don't be quiet."

Alice added, "Don't upset him - it is his birthday."

They stopped at the crossroads. Alice looked at the road sign, but she did not know which way to go.

Suddenly, there was a rumbling in the hedgerow and a head popped up. It was Colin the mole. Alice asked him which way it was to the Zoo. Colin took off his hat and scratched his head.

"You don't know do you?" Alfie said.

"Yes, I do, I just have some flees in my fur; they must have come from the Circus, or they could have come from the Zoo."

As he scratched his head the flees flew off towards the sun.

"Quick, let's follow them," said Alice and off they all went, with Ted still moaning about the bumpy ride.

Colin the mole was digging his hole, just popping up now and again for air and to make sure he was on the right track.

After a while the fleas were so far ahead they disappeared out of sight.

Then Colin the mole popped up and scratched his head. There was one more flea left on his head and off he flew.

Alice and *Alfie* followed round the bend and down a very steep hill. At the bottom there were big metal gates and a very tall fence. On the gates there was a sign saying 'ZOO, HOW DO YOU DO.'

Outside the gates there were a lot of people queuing to get in. The children were carrying their rag dolls and teddies with them and did not have to pay to get in.

Alice said to *Alfie*, "How are we going to get in? We have nobody to help us." Just then Mr. Mole popped up from his hole still scratching his head, but not a flea in sight, only a very sore bite.

Colin said, "I heard your plight," then with all his might he started digging. The soil was flying up in the air and before they could blink he was up on the other side of the fence.

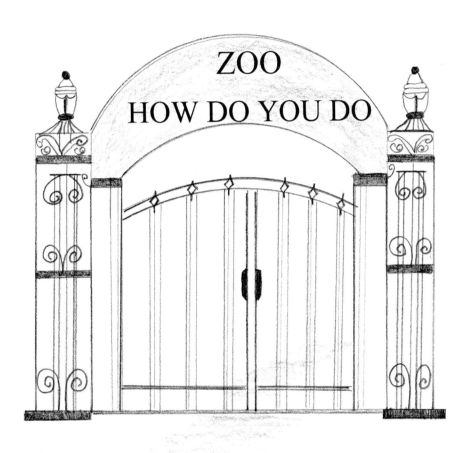

Colin shouted, "In you all come." *Alice, Alfie* and Ted crawled along the tunnel until they were in the Zoo. "Thank you," they all said, especially Ted as it was his treat.

They dusted themselves off and went off to have a look. The first thing they saw were the giraffes standing so tall. They were more surprised at seeing the rag dolls and a teddy bear walking and talking.

The next thing they saw were kangaroos bouncing up and down. *Alfie* thought he would try but it hurt his feet. The next attractions they saw were the lions, tigers and Mr. & Mrs. Hippopotamus.

They decided to sit down and have their lunch. *Alice* laid the blanket out on the ground and Ted opened his pot of honey. They all wished him "HAPPY BIRTHDAY."

There was a noise coming from the other side of the trees. It was a noise that Ted had heard before and all went to have a look. There, lying under the trees, were three big bears. *Alice* said to Ted, "They are very big, how much honey must they have eaten?"

Ted walked over to the three bears and took the lid off his honey pot and gave it to them.

Alice, Alfie and Ted carried on looking round the Zoo.

They saw every animal that lived on the planet apart from Nellie the elephant. *Alice* said, "She must be away with the Circus, I hope we will see her one day."

They all crawled back through under the fence and all the way home were talking about the animals. They all agreed that they were lucky to be free and not caged in. *Alfie* said, "The animals are all happy and get fed every day, because in the wild they may not have survived."

When they arrived back at the magic windmill they were very tired, and their feet had blisters, apart from Ted's - he just had a sore bottom from the cart. *Alfie* told him that he was lucky. Ted said, "It is by birthday you know." He kept telling them all night until he finally dropped off to sleep in a heap.

Alice and *Alfie* went upstairs to bed. The Moon shone down, and *Alice* opened the window. The Moon said, "I saw you today with all the animals in the Zoo. They may be caged but they are all saved, for children to see as if they were free. Sleep tight and don't let the bugs bite".

Alice, "I dig Colin the mole."

Alice and *Alfie*

THE TAKE AWAY

Jacques was going away for a few days to see his friend Monsieur Blanc at the Chateau. Before he left he whispered to *Alice* and *Alfie*, "You're in charge." After Jacques had left Ted asked, "In charge of what?"

Alice told him it was just a saying. Ted replied, "Well you are not in charge of me," and went off in a huff.

Alfie mumbled, "Hopefully, he will be gone all day."

Alice looked at *Alfie* and told him he looked scruffy, "Why don't I wash your clothes and clean your boots?"

Alfie replied, "That is a good idea, thank you." So he took off all of his clothes and *Alice* laughed, he looked so funny in this birthday suit with his rag arms and legs flopping around.

Alfie went and sat in the rocking chair and *Alice* looked at her clothes and thought to herself, "Mine need washing too." She put them all in the washing machine and switched it on. Then she laughed and said, "Do you remember *Alfie* when we were put in the washing machine?"

"Yes I do, this time it is a pleasure." He replied.

After the machine had finished *Alice* went outside and hung all the clothes on the line, while *Alfie* cleaned their boots and satchels.

Alice was just walking into the kitchen when a little scooter roared into the yard.

Alfie said, "No scooters round here."

They both hid behind the rocking chair as a little man with a funny helmet on his head walked into the kitchen and shouted, "Bonjour, take away."

Alfie whispered to *Alice*, "He wants to take us away."

"No way, especially without our clothes on," she replied.

The man walked over to the table and put very slim large boxes on the table. He mumbled to himself and went outside, jumped on his scooter and off he went.

Alfie walked over to the kitchen table and *Alice* asked, "What are in the boxes *Alfie*?"

"I don't know, but they feel very hot," he replied.

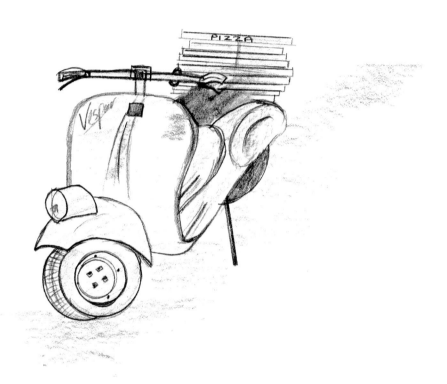

PIZZA

Vespa

On top of the two boxes it read 'PIZZA HAVE A NICE DAY.

Alfie opened the first box, and there inside was a hot flat bread thing with mushrooms, cheese and tomato.
The second box had all kinds of fish. *Alfie* just licked his lips. *Alice* said, "We can't! They must be for Jacques."

"But he is not here, and neither is Ted, thank goodness." *Alfie* replied.

Alice closed the lids on the boxes and went to fetch their clothes off the line as she knew they would be dry. *Alfie* shouted outside to her, "What about the pizza?"

Alice told him that if Jacques was not back by tea time they could eat them. *Alfie* starred up at the Moon and just prayed.

As *Alice* was taking the clothes off the line Ted arrived back at the magic windmill. He was very hungry after his long walk. He saw *Alice* and *Alfie* in their birthday suits and had a good chuckle to himself and went into the windmill.

95

The door shut behind him and he smelt the pizza as soon as he walked in. Ted picked up one of the boxes, went over to the rocking chair, lifted the lid and started munching.

Alfie and *Alice* did not see Ted arrive back.
They were walking across the yard when the pizza man came flying into the yard and nearly knocked *Alice* and *Alfie* over. They just fell to the floor on the cold paving.

The pizza man went over to the back door and tried to open it but the door was shut and locked.

He shouted through the letter box, "Please can I have my pizzas back? It was the wrong address, they should have gone to the magic castle down the road." The pizza man heard no reply and was very upset. He shouted through the letter box, "I hope you all feel bad." He jumped onto his scooter and off he went again.

Alice and *Alfie* jumped up. "Well, look, we were very clean until we fell to the floor," *Alice* said. They went to the back door and tried to open it but it was definitely locked.

They went around the side of the windmill and *Alfie* went up the ladder.

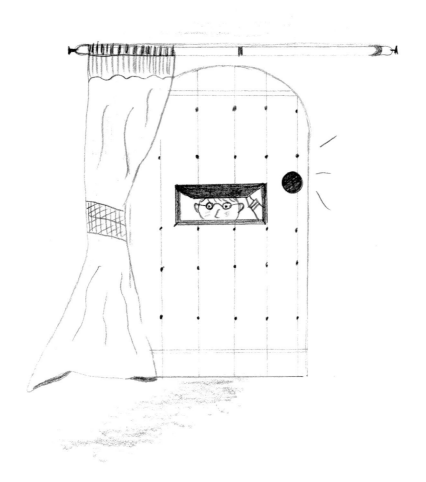

He shouted down to *Alice*, "We are locked out. The window is shut tight." He came back down the ladder and sat thinking what they could do to get back in. *Alice* said, "Ted will be back soon perhaps he will be able to think of a way in.

It started to get dark and still no Ted or Jacques. They were worried thinking what might have happened to Ted. They decided to go and look for him, but he was nowhere to be seen, so they decided to sleep in the old barn for the night.

Alfie said to *Alice*, "I could just eat that pizza now, I can almost taste it."

Alice replied, "I don't believe your thinking about your stomach, *Alfie*. What about poor old Ted out there all on his own? He must be very hungry and tired."

Inside the windmill Ted had just woken up after a lovely snooze. He got up and had a look round but could not see *Alice* and *Alfie*. He saw the second pizza on the table and started again.

Just then the mice came running in crying out, "Pizza, pizza, our favourite."

Ted looked at them, then the pizza and he really did not feel very well, so he gave them a large slice and then he fell asleep.

The next morning when Ted woke he could still not see the rag dolls, so he decided to go and have a look for them. He walked down to the bridge, then all the way to the magic castle. Outside the door he saw a note which read, 'NO PIZZAS HAVE BEEN EATEN BY OTHERS AT THE MAGIC WINDMILL, WILL BRING ORDER BACK TONIGHT SIGNED PIZZA MAN.'

Ted did not understand what was happening but decided pizza again for tea if he came back at the right time.

Ted walked all the way back and just as he reached the yard at the windmill *Alice* and *Alfie* were coming out of the barn.

Alice shouted, "You poor old thing you must be very tired and hungry. Where have you been?"

Ted replied, "Well," then he thought he should just keep quiet.

Alfie answered, "We have been locked out all night, the windmill door locked and there are two pizzas inside on the table with our names on them."

Ted looked surprised and asked, "What are pizzas? I don't know what you mean." So *Alice* explained what had happened. Ted said, "Well now I understand."

Alfie suggested, "If we take our ladder at the side of the windmill and put it up to the gutter on the other side, then Ted could climb over the roof and drop down the chimney, then open the door."

Ted pleaded, "Please, don't make me do that! It sounds too dangerous." *Alfie* shouted at him, "Father Christmas does it once every year, so why can you not do it just once?"

So, up Ted went. He sat on the top of the chimney and shouted down, "I can't, I can't." Just at that moment Mr. Magpie was flying past and flew straight into Ted and pushed him down the chimney.

Alice and *Alfie* applauded Mr. Magpie who flew off with a loud cry.

Meanwhile Ted had landed in the fire grate. He was covered in soot from head to toe. He unlocked the back door and *Alice* and *Alfie* walked in.

Alice said, "I think it is washing machine time for you," and chucked him into the machine, switched it on and round he went.

103

Alfie cried out, "*Alice* look the pizzas have all gone, not one piece left." Ted was watching out of the washing machine door and could see them looking at the boxes and kept his head down.

The washing machine finished, and out Ted fell. *Alice* picked him up and hung him out to dry. After a while she fetched him back in. Ted sat at the table looking at *Alfie* who was still shocked at the missing pizzas.

Ted had a very red face and said, "What's with the boxes? They are all empty!"

Just at that moment the mice came running in with cheese and tomatoes all over their chins. *Alice* shouted, "How could you have eaten so much?"

Just as the mice were going to squeak Ted shouted, "CAT," and the mice ran away.

Alice said, "Well they definitely had the take away." Nothing else was said, thankfully for Ted.

That night Ted went to supper at the magic castle, but only in his dreams.

The Moon laughed watching Ted drop off to sleep.

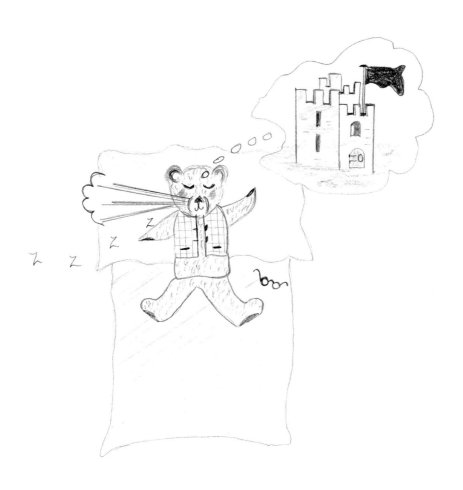

105

Alfie, Ted's dreaming of pizza, SHAME!"

Alice and *Alfie*

PENNIES FROM HEAVEN

107

After the takeaway Ted was still feeling ill. *Alice* and *Alfie* had cleaned up before Jacques came home.

After a good night's sleep, Jacques had got up early and was outside in the barn working.

Alice said to *Alfie*, "What is he doing?" He was sawing and hammering, and at the end of the day the noise stopped when Jacques went in for his tea.

Alice whispered to *Alfie*, "Let us go and have a look at what he has been doing."

They went down the ladder and ran across to the barn. On the door was a note saying, 'BEWARE WET PAINT.'

Alfie whispered to *Alice*, "It is dry."

Alice opened the door and they went in. It was quite dark, so they turned the lights on. They could smell the paint in the air. There was a table with a box which had a lovely wooden roof, and at the front there were three holes with wooden ledges underneath. At the side of the windows were little shutters. It had been painted in the same colour as the windmill.

Alfie touched the box, and yes, the note was right: it was wet, and his arm was covered in green paint.

Alice said, "You silly billy." She tried to get the paint off, but no, it was on for good.

Alfie scratched his head and asked, "What is the box for?"

Alice said, "Perhaps it is for mice." Up in the roof of the barn sat Mr. and Mrs. Owl. They had been trying to get to sleep. Mr. Owl flew down, looked at *Alice* and *Alfie* and said, "if we tell you what it is for, will you turn the lights off, so we can all go back to sleep."

Alice replied, "Of course."

Mr. Owl screeched out, "It is a bird box for the windmill wall."

Alfie asked, "What sort of birds?"

Mrs. Owl shouted down, "Any birds that can fit through the hole. Now please turn off the lights."

Alice and *Alfie* turned off the lights and went back to the windmill, up the ladder and sat on the window seat. They went off to sleep dreaming of what birds would be flying into the box.

111

Alfie dreamt of crows, but they would be too big for the holes. *Alice* dreamt of the seagulls, but they live at the seaside.

The next morning, they were both awoken by more noise. *Alfie* looked out of the window and there was Jacques with the bird box and a big hammer. He had climbed all the way up the ladder and was fitting the bird box right next to their window. Afterwards he went back to have his breakfast.

Ted said, "What's with the box?"

Alfie told him they were waiting for new visitors. Ted replied, "It looks good for pigeons and their post."

Downstairs they heard Jacques on the phone to his friend Kimmy. She told him she would be over to look at the bird box later.

When Kimmy arrived a pair of robins were looking at the box, but it was not for them and they flew off.

Kimmy stood looking up at the bird box and told Jacques that she would like one. It was brilliant.

Jacques told her how much it would cost, and she said, "That is fine, I think you would sell so many at the Farmers Market next week."

Jacques said, "It will be like pennies from heaven, another string to my bow."

After coffee Kimmy left, and Jacques went back into the barn to make some more bird boxes.

Every day birds arrived at the box at the top of the ladder, but decided it was not a home for them. Then early one morning *Alice* and *Alfie* were awoken by a noise they had not heard before. They both looked out of the window. There were two little birds flying in and out of the box.

Alice opened the window and shouted, "What's with all the noise?" The birds stopped and told *Alice* they were so excited about finding their new home.

Alfie asked them, "What sort of birds are you as we have never seen you before?"

The birds replied, "Swallows, we have come all the way from England."

Alice asked, "Do you know Nichole? She lives in England?"

"No, we only know Jack and Jill. They are two windmills where we live."

"We decided to go on holiday and this is where we have ended up. We are so tired so if you don't mind we are going to get some sleep." So they flew into the bird box and not a sound was heard until tea time.

Jacques saw the swallows and was over the moon that they had arrived. He took pictures of them, and *Alice* and *Alfie* were in the photos too, together with Ted with his tongue out.

Jacques sent some of the pictures to Nichole back in England. Jacques put the letter on the kitchen table ready to post. *Alice* saw the envelope and said to *Alfie*, "I hope it is to ask Nichole to come back for a holiday."

The rag dolls went out to the barn to see how Jacques was getting on. There were bird boxes everywhere, some still wet with paint, and some with price tags on, ready for the Farmers Market.

The next morning Kimmy phoned, and *Alfie* heard Jacques say, "Yes, today is the day."

Alfie ran into the bedroom and shouted to *Alice*, "Today is the Farmers Market, can we go?"

"Of course," replied *Alice*.

They ran outside and jumped into the bucket in the back of the van. Ted was running and tripped over, just as Jacques was coming out of the barn with the last of the bird boxes. He saw Ted on the floor, picked him up and dusted him off; he was going to take him for good luck.

Jacques put Ted up on the dashboard in the front of the van.

Alfie looked at *Alice* and said, "I don't believe it, Ted has done it again, he's in the front."

When they reached the Farmers Market, Kimmy was waiting with the table. As they were displaying the bird boxes the butcher's wife said, "I will have one of those, please." This went on all morning until all twenty had been sold.

Jacques was so pleased that he had another new talent for making money in his old age. So, every week he would go to a different market with his boxes.

Back at the windmill the baby swallows had hatched, and *Alice* and *Alfie* thought it was such fun with a new family at the magic windmill, and Jacques had put up so many bird boxes it was a bird village in the air.

Jacques had built an amazing bird table and every day Ted was there looking for nuts.

Alice and *Alfie* thanked the Moon and Nichole's star for the new arrivals. The birds' song was so sweet, a lot more than just a tweet, but they had to watch out for the mess on their feet.

Alfie said, "I would love to see Jack and Jill."

Alice and *Alfie*

RETURN TO SENDER

Summer had arrived, and everybody was happy, even Ted. Jacques was still selling fruit and veg from the magic garden and he was still making bird boxes. He was even busier now than when he made flour in the mill.

Alice had decided to write a letter to Nichole. She sat at the window watching the ducks on the water.

Alfie came into the room and said to *Alice*, "What are we doing today?"

"Ssssh, I am writing a letter to Nichole," she shouted.

Alfie grunted, "Why? She never replies!"

Alice told *Alfie* to take Ted out and find something for them to do. Anything, but something that would not disturb her writing.

Alfie went downstairs and grabbed Ted, "Come on, we are going to have an adventure," he told him.

As they walked into the yard Ted shouted, "You are hurting my arm." So *Alfie* dropped him, and Ted landed in a puddle.

Ted shouted, "That's not a nice adventure."

Alfie said, "Come on, let's go."

Alfie and Ted went into the barn and got out the old tandem bike. *Alfie* jumped on and Ted got on the back, but Ted could not reach the pedals because he was too short. *Alfie* pedalled away and off they went.
Ted was soon dry with the wind blowing through his fur.

Alice was busy writing her letter which read:

> Dear Nichole,
> I wish you were here, we are all
> missing you now we are back at
> the magic windmill. I'm sorry we
> ran away at Christmas, well skied
> away. The windmill is still making
> its magic and Jacques is fine.
> Alfie has gone bike riding with Ted,
> I hope they come back in one piece!
> Every night I draw a picture of Mr.
> Moon, sometimes he's lying on his
> back, and sometimes he's full of
> himself, shining so bright you don't
> even need a light.
> Love Alice, Alfie and Ted xxx

Alice put the letter in an envelope and put Nichole's address on it, which she got from downstairs from an old letter to Jacques, and she wrote her address on the back. She wrote on the back, 'From, *Alice*, *Alfie* and Ted, the Magic Windmill, France.' Then she walked off to the village to post it in the box.

Meanwhile, *Alfie* and Ted were in a bit of a spin. They had gone to the village green and ended up on the roundabout in the children's park. Ted was trying hard to stay on as *Alfie* was pushing it faster and faster. Then they both went flying off, landing on their heads.

As they got up and brushed themselves off they saw *Alice* walking past. *Alfie* shouted, "Where are you off to?"

She replied, "The post office, to post my letter to Nichole back in England."

Alfie shouted, "She won't get it, just like last time!"

Alice arrived at the post box and before she posted the letter she said a little prayer, "Please Nichole, reply soon," and kissed the envelope and posted it into the box.

129

The boys arrived, that is *Alfie* and Ted. *Alfie* said to *Alice*, "Jump on, let's go for a spin." Ted sat on the handlebars and off they went.

Alice shouted, "Home James, home."

Ted said, "Who's James?"

"Just a saying," said *Alice*.

When they eventually got back to the magic windmill the postman was just leaving. They all hid behind the barn until he was out of sight.

Jacques was still out. They all walked into the kitchen and there on the door mat were some letters. *Alice* picked them up and she said, "All bills."

"Oh yes, you are right." Replied *Alfie*. *Alice* put the letters onto the table, with Nichole's on the top.

Jacques was late coming home that night from La Rochelle where he had a market stall on the harbour front. He had 'caught the sun,' which Ted could not understand.

He said to *Alice*, "How could Jacques have caught the sun? Were they playing a game?"

Alice replied, "No, I'm afraid it is another one of those sayings."

Ted just scratched his head.

Jacques did not open his letters before he went to bed and left them on the kitchen table. Ted stayed up late watching the T.V. and had decided to have some of his favourite food, honey. He looked in the cupboard and yes, there was a new jar. He tried to open it, but the lid was stuck. He got a knife out the drawer and tried to prise the lid off. But no luck.

He sat at the table very upset, just looking at the jar. He heard voices coming from the curtain next to the door of the magic garden. He went over and pulled back the curtains. It was the mice laughing at him.

Ted said, "It is not funny with no honey for my tummy."

The mice jumped up onto the table and one of them knocked over the jar and the lid fell off and the honey ran out all over the table, covering the letters.

"What a mess!" Ted cried.

The mice ran away, leaving him to clear up all the mess.

Ted spooned up all the honey that he could. The letters were in a terrible state and he tried to clean them the best he could.

The top letter had opened from all the rubbing and cleaning. It was the letter from Nichole. With honey on his paws the letter became a sticky mess, so he decided to put them all in the bin and then cleaned the kitchen table.

Jacques was up and out very early as he had a very busy day again.

Alice and *Alfie* came downstairs.

Alice said, "Where are all the letters and bills?"

Alfie looked around but could not find them. Ted was in the bed box and heard them and just covered his ears.

Alfie said, "Perhaps Jacques had read them and put them in the bin."

There was a noise outside in the yard; it was the dustman. *Alice* shouted out, "Oh no," but it was too late – the rubbish had all gone. She came back inside and just wept and wept and wept.

Ted went to his bed knowing what he had done. All morning *Alfie* tried to stop *Alice* from crying. She did after a while, and then she realised that her letter was well on the way to England.

The next morning, they heard the letter box open. *Alfie* ran downstairs and there on the mat was a little letter. It was the one from *Alice* to Nichole. *Alfie* took it back upstairs to her, and she started crying again.

On the front was a large red stamp. It read 'RETURN TO SENDER.'

She asked *Alfie*, "What does that mean?"

Alfie replied, "No idea, but at least you have your letter back."

The next morning when the postman turned up at the front door, *Alice* ran over to his bike and popped her letter in his sack. But yes, the very next day back it came.

Later that night they heard Jacques downstairs singing "Chanson D'Amour, ra da da da da."

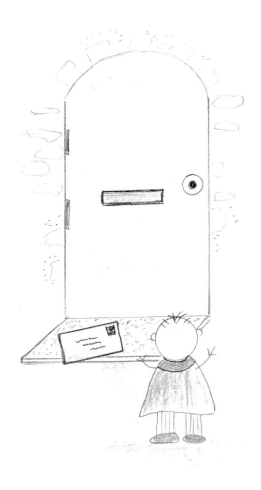

When he had gone to bed, they all went downstairs and, on the table, there was a letter that he had written to his friend Monsieur Blanc. Jacques had left a pouch of French stamps and on the letter was a stamp in the top right-hand corner.

Alice then realised you needed one of these sticky labels to post a letter. So she ran upstairs and got her letter and stuck one of these sticky labels on, just like Jacques.

Alice looked over at Ted and said, "You had better be good while I'm gone." Then she ran all the way to the post box with the Moon shining down for her to see the way.

139

Alice told Ted, "Be good or get stamped."

Alice and *Alfie*

SUITED AND BOOTED

Alice waited for the postman every morning, but no post from England.

The summer was very hot, and Jacques was very tired. He had been so busy, and Kimmy had suggested a holiday. A very special holiday, a holiday on a barge.

Alice and *Alfie* heard them talking about the holiday but did not understand what a barge was.

One sunny morning Jacques was on the phone. He said to Kimmy, "I will see you at ten thirty." He had packed two suitcases that were by the back door, and a pair of old boots.

Alice, *Alfie* and Ted were fast asleep in their bed box when Kimmy arrived. They woke as the back door opened. Kimmy asked Jacques, "Are you suitcased and booted?"

"Yes," replied Jacques.

Alice coughed. Jacques and Kimmy looked across the room. "What was that?" said Kimmy.

Jacques' replied, "It must be the fire going out." He went across and checked the fire guard was in place.

Jacques said to Kimmy, "I am going to take *Alice* and *Alfie* with us. They will love the barge.

142

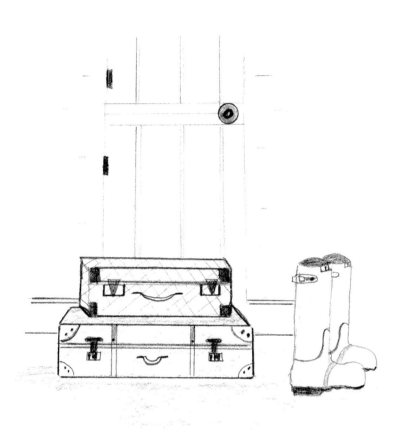

143

Jacques told Kimmy, "I have left some food in the fridge for our guests."

Alice looked at *Alfie* and said, "What guests?" *Alfie* just shrugged his shoulders.

Jacques picked *Alice* and *Alfie* up and popped them into an old basket. Then they all left, leaving Ted fast asleep at the bottom of the bed box.

When Ted eventually woke up, *Alice* and *Alfie* had gone. Just a note on the table which he could not read. He did not care; it was lovely, the peace and quiet.

Jacques and Kimmy arrived at the river. It was somewhere that *Alice* and *Alfie* had never been before.

There were very large boats tied up alongside the riverbank.

Jacques and Kimmy took their cases out of the back of the van and carried them onto the first boat.

They both put their old boots on. Kimmy chuckled, "There we are, suitcased and booted, as they say."

Jacques said, "Now have we got everything?"

"Yes," replied Kimmy.

145

Alice whispered to *Alfie*, "They have forgotten us!"

Alfie lifted his arm up and it went down on the hooter of the van. "Beep, beep, beep," it went.

Jacques looked back and said to himself, "What is going on?" He walked over to the old van and looked inside. There was *Alfie* lying across the steering wheel. He unlocked the door and scratched his head thinking, "*Alice* and *Alfie* must be more than just toys."

He put them back into the basket and locked the van and walked back to the old boat. He whispered to them, "Now this is our home for two weeks." He jumped on board and put *Alice* and *Alfie* up front in the cabin windows. He told them, "You are the look outs."

As he walked away *Alfie* said to *Alice*, "What are we looking out for?"

"No idea," she replied, "But I do know one thing – no Ted for two weeks."

Alfie grinned and said, "That is the best news of the day."

147

Jacques started the engine. Kimmy untied the barge and off they floated.

Alice and *Alfie* had a pleasant view ahead but could not work out what they were looking out for!

Back at the magic windmill Ted was getting very lonely. He just slept, ate, slept and ate. Then early one morning the back door opened. He popped his head up out of the bed box expecting *Alice* and *Alfie*, but no, it was Nichole, her husband and their son Tom.

They put their cases down and put the kettle on.

Nichole said to her husband Frank, "What do you think about the windmill? Is it just as you imagined?"

"Yes, it is, and more. I could definitely live here when I retire from the Army. No more going away would be magic and this would be the place to live."

Nichole was so pleased he liked the windmill.

Nichole told Tom to go and find *Alice* and *Alfie*. He ran upstairs and shouted down, "No, they are not up here."

Nichole noticed some movement in the bed box. She lifted the cover and there was Ted. She lifted him out; he was dirty from head to paws! Ted did not move.

Tom came back downstairs, and Nichole told him that she had found him in the bed box, but no *Alice* and *Alfie*.

Frank had gone outside to have a look around. He sat by the riverbank thinking to himself, "What a beautiful place to live."

Tom cuddled Ted, which pleased him as he was so fed up with being left on his own.

Every night Ted would look up at the Moon and ask for *Alice* and *Alfie* to return. He told Ted, "They are having fun, but they will be back home at the weekend. So, have fun too, and don't look sad because Tom loves you too."

Meanwhile, Jacques and Kimmy had arrived on the barge at La Rochelle. What a place, boats everywhere and lots of nice smells, and bells ringing.

The barge had to be turned around, so they could go back. If only it was on a track. Jacques had decided to go a different way back with lots of locks and, definitely, knocks.

The barge arrived at the first lock. *Alice* said, "It is like a big tank filling up with water! I hope we don't sink."

Then the big gates were opened by a man turning a wheel. As they floated out of the tank Jacques thanked the Lock Master. Every hour was another lock until the barge did dock.

Jacques said to Kimmy, "We will stay here tonight. Look, that Café up on the riverbank will suit us just fine."

Jacques and Kimmy got suited and booted and went to the little Café for their meal, leaving *Alice* and *Alfie* with a knife and an apple to peel.

Alfie said, "I will be glad when we are back at the magic windmill to have a rest. Holidays, what's it all about?"

Alice and *Alfie* fell asleep dreaming of Ted, wondering what he had been eating back at the windmill.

It was Nichole's last day and Tom was out playing. He took Ted with him, dragging him by his paws. Tom saw an old boat next to the bridge and jumped on. He pretended he was a pirate.

Tom tied Ted to the top of the sail and hoisted it up, shouting to him to look out. The sun was very hot, and Ted's head dropped.

Nichole shouted out to Tom, "Supper is ready and early to bed as we are leaving early in the morning."

Poor old Ted was still tied up on top of the sail. He could not untie the knot. When it got dark the Moon shone down and had a good laugh. He told Ted not to worry as *Alice* and *Alfie* would be back in the morning, and off the Moon floated to tell the rag dolls about Ted's plight.

The Moon shone as bright as he could, and *Alice* woke up and smiled. The Moon told her, "Ted is all tied up, and in deep water too."

The next morning Nichole's bags were packed, and Frank loaded them into the car. They all said goodbye to the magic windmill and the car drove off down the lane with Ted shouting, "Get me down!" but there was nobody around.

When Nichole reached the crossroads, she turned off to the left and Jacques came around the bend from the right. They had just missed each other by thirty seconds.

155

Alice and *Alfie* were back home at the magic windmill, and off they went to bed.

The Moon was shining down, and *Alice* looked out of the window and told him, "I have a funny feeling Nichole has been here."

The Moon replied, "Yes, you are right, but don't forget Ted's plight; he is still up the mast in the moonlight."

Alice and *Alfie* ran down to the riverbank and yes, there he was, shouting out, "I'm the Captain of the ship, now get me down so I can have something to eat."

Alice said, "Did you know Nichole has been here?"

"Yes, for nearly two weeks," he replied.

All night *Alice* cried. *Alfie* told her, "At least she came back, and not her letter!"

Alice dropped off to sleep counting fluffy sheep, while Ted was learning French from a little phrase book. So funny!"

"*Alice*, I really need a holiday!"

Alice and *Alfie*

BEE HIVE YOURSELF

Alice was still very upset about missing Nichole.

Alfie said, "Perhaps she will come back at Christmas time. You know they like skiing, and their skis are still here."

Alice wiped a tear from her eye, "Thank you, *Alfie*, that has given me a whole lot to look forward to."

Jacques was out in his barn making bird boxes and had set up a stall at the end of the lane.

Ted was downstairs in the kitchen and he had been stung by a bee on his nose as he was being too nosey again.

Alfie asked him, "Where have you been to get stung?"

Ted replied, "Down by the river and over the bridge, out in the fields where the lavender is growing. It smells incredible and the bees are flying everywhere. I thought there would be honey there, but none to be seen, just a sting on the nose."

Alice put some cream on it to cool it down.

At the end of the day Jacques came in for his tea.
Alice, *Alfie* and Ted were in their bed box.

160

Jacques picked up the phone and started talking. He said, "I've finished the hive; now we should get plenty of honey," then went up to bed. Ted's ears pricked up at the sheer mention of honey.

Alice asked *Alfie*, "What is a hive?"

Alfie replied, "No idea, but it sounds like it could be in the barn. Let us go and have a look." They crept out, trying not to disturb Ted.

Out in the barn on the table was a large box which had shutters that looked just like the windows around the windmill.

Jacques had painted it in the same colours as the windmill. And yes, again *Alfie* got paint on him – he just had to touch.

Alice looked all around the box and whispered to *Alfie*, "Where is the honey, nowhere to be seen?"

Mr. Owl was looking down from the beams above and screeched, "Lights on again. We are trying to sleep."

Alfie asked him, "Have you seen the bees?"

Mr. Owl replied, "What bees?"

162

163

Alfie shouted back up, "The bees that live in the hive."

Mrs. Owl looked down from the oak beam and told them, "The bees are outside, and the hives should be too!"

Alfie shouted back up, "O.k."

So, *Alice* and *Alfie* lifted the hive off the table, paint and all.

They dropped it on the ground outside the barn doors.

Alfie turned the lights off and shut the barn doors.

Alice and *Alfie* sat on the step with the Moon shining down. *Alice* asked *Alfie*, "I wonder what time the bees will turn up?"

The Moon was napping, woke up and had a little chuckle. He told them, "Not until daylight and only when the sun is rising." So, they both sat there, waiting. Suddenly the sun poked his head out and started to rise over the hill.

Then the back door opened. It was Jacques. *Alice* and *Alfie* just lay there not making a sound.

Jacques walked across to the barn and rubbed his eyes and said to himself, "How did the hive get here? Did I, or didn't I?" Then he noticed *Alice* and *Alfie* lying on the floor. He picked them up and took them back to the windmill.

"Now you two, back in your bed box. Rag dolls moving around, and hives too." He was muttering to himself.

"Now you all behive yourselves!"

After breakfast he carried the beehive out towards the woods. *Alice* and *Alfie* followed and made sure he did not see them.

Ted was running behind thinking, "Honey, honey for my tummy."

Jacques stopped right at the end of the forest and out in front of him was the large lavender field. He took the roof off the top of the hive and dropped in wooden frames, then placed the roof back on.

Jacques spoke to the hive and said, "Now do your best."

Alfie asked *Alice*, "What are they for?"

"No idea," she replied.

Jacques went back to the windmill while *Alice* and *Alfie* waited patiently.

Then one bee flew up out of the lavender and hovered around the hive. Then another, and another. One went up into the shutters at the side of the hive. He crawled in, out of sight.

Next a very large bee squeezed itself in between the shutters. It was all too much excitement for Ted who went over to have a look. And yes, you can guess what happened. A bee flew out of the hive, saw Ted and stung him on his nose.

"Not again!" he shouted, running around like a mad Ted.

Alice told him to behive himself. *Alice* laughed, and the bees flew back into the lavender fields. That was that, and nothing happened all day.

They all went back home with nothing, only Ted with a sore nose so *Alice* put cream on Ted's nose again. Then it was time for bed.

The next morning Jacques was up early and went back to the hive.

Alice and *Alfie* followed, but not Ted. He was still hurting in bed.

Jacques opened the hive, but still no bees inside.
This went on for more than a week and not even a bee in sight.

The next morning Ted was out on one of his 'fed up walks.' He ended up in the village. So he decided to go to the baker. He walked to the back door and lying on the floor, was a tray of iced buns. He licked his lips and grabbed one, running off to the park.

He was out of breath and sat down on the bottom of the slide. He put his iced bun down just for a moment and, just as he went to pick it up, to his amazement there was a bee that had flown down from the tree. He was eating Ted's iced bun, which Ted decided was not much fun. Ted flicked it away, but it flew back down.

Ted moved away and so did the bee. Ted started to run, but so did the bee. As he looked around there were three. He was running as fast as his little legs would go and by now there was a big black cloud; hundreds and hundreds of bees were flying from the trees.

171

Ted ran all the way to the hive. When he got there his iced bun flew up into the air and landed on the floor. He sat there and watched while the bees ate his lunch. Then he saw the large bee fly out from the hive and it flew all around the other bees. One by one they followed the large bee back into the hive.

Just at that moment Mr. Owl flew past and shouted to Ted, "I see the Queen bee has arrived."

All day Ted sat and watched the bees going in and out of the hive collecting the nectar from the lavender in the field.

Early one morning Jacques turned up at the hive, all dressed up in white nets, with a smoke tin. He puffed away at the side of the hive making the bees sleepy. Then gradually lifted out one of the wooden trays scraping all the honey into the bin, leaving drips and drops which turned into lots.

Ted watched as Jacques walked away, then licked his lips and had a field day. The honey was so good. But one bee saw him licking the honey and yes, the chase was on again.

Back at the windmill *Alice* said, "Look on the table Ted, lots of honey."

Ted replied, "That's not funny," and went off to bed.

"*Alice*, that was a sticky end for Ted!"

Alice and *Alfie*

TIME WILL TELL

Early one morning there was a noise that *Alfie* and *Alice* had not heard before. It was as if someone was whistling a tune to a song.

Alice looked out of the window and at the side of the ladder she saw three little heads sticking out of the bird box. The swallows were making a very loud noise which upset Ted. They were calling for food.

Every now and again Mum and Dad would come flying back with food in their beaks for their young. Then back off again to collect more food.

Ted said to *Alice*, "How long is this going to go on for?"

She replied, "For quite a few weeks yet." Ted just covered his ears with his paws and went off to sleep.

Later that afternoon there was a clip clop sound in the yard. It was the Rag and Bone man.

Jacques went outside to see him and said, "Hello Mr. Rag. You are working late."

"Yes, there were a lot more rags to collect from the village this time," he replied.

Jacques asked him where he was staying tonight.

He told Jacques, "Underneath the stars!"

Alice heard and whispered to *Alfie*, "I wonder if it is Nichole's star?"

Jacques told him he could put the horse and cart in the barn and he was welcome to stay at the windmill.

After the horse was settled down for the evening, Mr. Rag went into the windmill for his supper.

Jacques and Mr. Rag were talking about their past into the early hours.

Alice, Alfie and Ted were upset because they could not watch the T.V. and went upstairs to bed.

The next morning Mr. Rag fed his horse and was ready to go onto the next town. He shouted to Jacques, "Look, just a small gesture for letting me stay the night." He handed over three jackets to Jacques. They were all in very good condition. One was made from tartan and looked brand new.

Jacques thanked him and as he waved Mr. Rag off a shiny silver object dropped out of the pocket of the tartan jacket. It fell onto the straw on the floor. Jacques did not notice this, but *Alice* did.

178

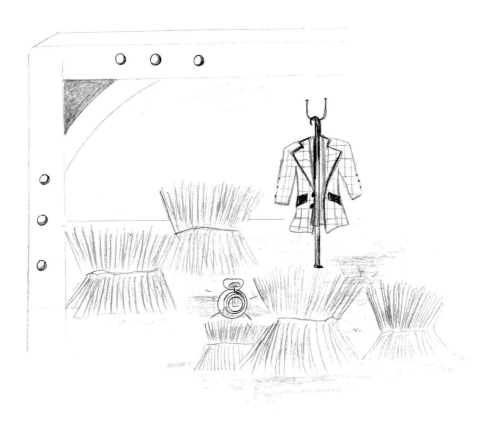

179

Alice waited until Jacques went back indoors, then she slid down the ladder and went over to the straw. She pushed the straw around until she found the shiny object. Then ran back to the ladder and up she went.

She cried out, "*Alfie*, look what I have found!" She told him that it had fallen out of an old jacket that Mr. Rag had given to Jacques.

They sat on the bed, *Alice* holding it in her hand. On the front of a round case was a picture and some writing. The picture was of a castle. *Alfie* read out the words, "It says Mclachlan Castle."

Alice unclipped the clasp on the side and it opened.

They both sat there speechless, which was very unusual.

At this point Ted woke up and walked over and had a look. He mumbled, "It's ticking."

Alfie replied, "We know, it is a watch."

They had never seen a watch like this before.

Alice said, "As it has fallen out of the jacket, I am going to call it a pocket watch."

Alfie said, "Look at the hands, they are going backwards. That is not what a clock does. Their hands go forward."

All the numbers had a picture underneath them. *Alice* thought the bagpipes were the best. *Alfie* loved the set of swords and Ted thought the fishing rods were brilliant.

Alice shut the lid and said to *Alfie*, "This is a very special watch; we must keep it safe."

Jacques had gone into the barn to work.

Alice and *Alfie* went downstairs to look at the clock and to compare it with the pocket watch.

Hanging over the rocking chair were the three jackets that Mr. Rag had given Jacques. The tartan one was on the top. *Alice* picked it up and there inside was a waistcoat fitted into the jacket. It had a long silver chain. She realised that this was what the watch must have been hanging on.

Alice took it off the waistcoat and clipped it to the pocket watch. On the inside of the jacket was a tag that read, 'The Mclachlan clan. Wash by hand.'

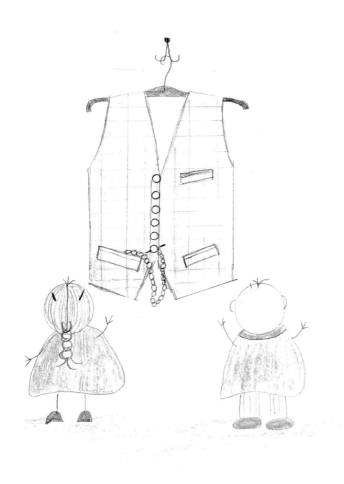

183

Alfie said, "Perhaps that is what we should have printed on us, 'No washing machine!'"

Alice and *Alfie* heard Jacques coming back into the windmill and ran upstairs.

They sat at the top of the stairs. Jacques walked in and muttered to himself, "I must clean the jackets."

Alfie was just about to shout out, "Not the washing machine," and *Alice* covered his mouth.

Jacques popped them into the washing machine and around they went.

An hour later Jacques took them out. The cotton jackets were clean, but they had all shrunk. Jacques just stood there and laughed. He chucked them in the corner with a couple of old sheets, ready for Mr. Rag on his next trip.

Later that night, after Jacques had gone to bed, *Alice* and *Alfie* came downstairs. *Alice* picked up the tartan jacket and put it on. It was just a little bit too big; *Alfie* thought it looked just fine. *Alice* clipped the watch and chain into the pocket.

Alfie said, "You look like a tartan princess."

Alice would not take the jacket off and went to bed with it on.

Alice and *Alfie* lay in the bed box, with Ted at the bottom wriggling around. Ted woke up and next to him was the watch, which had fallen out of the pocket. He opened the case. It lit up with a glow and the hands started spinning around backwards; they went so fast.

Alice and *Alfie* woke up. *Alice* said, "What is happening?"

Alfie whispered, "Time will tell."

They all kept looking at the watch and suddenly they were transported back in time. They had landed on a hillside full of heather.

Alice said, "It looks like number five on the watch."

As they started walking they noticed a castle in the distance. As they got closer they could see the flag flying with the name, 'Mclachlan Castle.'

Alfie said, "I wonder if it is magical?" They walked up to the Castle and across the drawbridge.

Alfie pulled the rope which rang a bell inside. He was so light he went flying into the air. He kept ringing the bell, but nobody answered.

Alice said, "The Castle must be empty." She looked at the watch and the hands had stopped and were pointing at the number eleven, the Mclachlan Castle. Then from the tower above they heard a voice.

"So you have brought my watch back and my tartan jacket; you have saved me." At the same time a man lowered a bucket on a rope and *Alice* dropped the jacket and watch into the pail and up it went.

After a while the big oak doors opened and a little old man with a white beard appeared. He asked *Alice* and *Alfie* to come inside, but not Ted. "Teds are bad luck."

Alfie said, "I know what you mean!"

Ted just shouted, "I did not want to come in anyway."

Alice and *Alfie* went inside and sat at the old kitchen table. The old man told them a story about another King from another Castle, who had put a curse on him, and the only way back to his time was the watch.

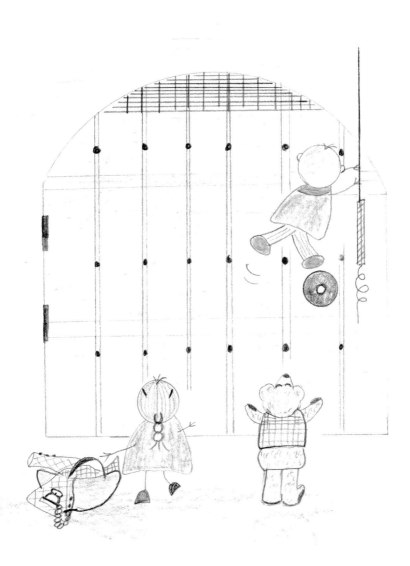

The old man told them that he had been in the tower for twenty-five years.

Alfie said, "What about food? How have you survived?"

The old man told them, "The white owls bring me food and water each day."

As the old man opened his watch, the jacket changed back to its original size.

He slipped it on and just at that moment the whole Castle came alive with men playing bagpipes and men dancing around swords.

Alice and *Alfie* asked him, "Do you know the Wooden Prince? He lives in a Castle near where we live."

"No, but one day I would like to meet him."

There was a loud knock at the door. The old man went over and opened it. It was Ted. He told the old man it was very rude to leave a person waiting at the front door.

The old man said, "No thank you," and shut the door.

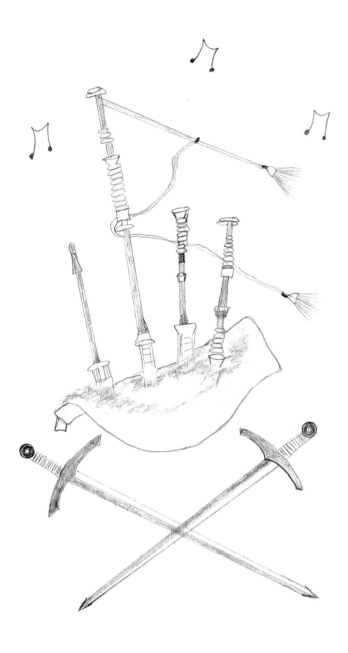

191

Alfie said, "Look, the watch, it has started to spin."

The old man put *Alice* and *Alfie* into the bucket and went over and opened the big oak doors, grabbed Ted and chucked him in with *Alice* and *Alfie*. The bucket flew up into the air, over the hills and far away.

Suddenly they all woke from their dream when Jacques hit the bed box with the hoover!

Alice whispered to *Alfie*, "I dreamt about a Castle."

Alfie replied, "So did I."

Alice asked, "Where is the jacket and the watch?"

Ted muttered, "It has gone back to another time!"

Alice was sad, "But will we ever see it again?"

Alfie said, "Time will tell."

That night the Moon said, "Tick tock, tick tock, time will repeat itself."

Alfie said, "There is no King, only I"

Alice and *Alfie*

THE PUZZLE

195

After the day with the watch, *Alice* and *Alfie* decided on a relaxing day, if that was possible.

Ted had gone out early looking for honey as he had no supplies left.

Alice said to *Alfie*, "Let us go and look at what Jacques had been up to in the barn." He had gone out early to sell bird boxes.

Alice and *Alfie* slid down the ladder and there was the bird box full of life.

The little swallows needed feeding. *Alice* told them, "Your Mum will be back soon, so you tweet as much as you like!"

In the barn on the large table were lots of pieces of wood. All were flat and unusual shapes. They could not work out what they were for. Some Jacques had painted on the edges. There was also a cube painted in cream. Yet again they had no idea what it was for.

Every day they would go out to the barn and Jacques had finished a bit more. Now the cube had numbers on it, one to six.

197

Alice picked it up and accidentally dropped it. It landed with the number one showing.

Alfie then dropped the cube and that landed on number three. He said, "I have won!"

They had a lovely time, each of them trying for the highest number. It was a good game.

Alice said, "What about all the funny shapes, what are they for?"

Alfie replied, "Look, Jacques has painted colours on them," but still they did not know what he was building.

In the corner was lots of wood, all assorted sizes, some old, some new. There was an old piece of wood which was shaped like a boat. *Alfie* picked it up and the bark was all different colours.

Alice asked *Alfie*, "Perhaps we could make a sailing boat?"

Alice found some old sheets stacked up in the corner of the barn.

Alfie cut some pieces of wood and found some glue and old rope.

Alfie put the boat together and *Alice* wrapped the sheets around the mast to make a sail. It was brilliant – they had made a small sailing boat.

They took it down to the river, and as they dropped into the water someone shouted, "Ouch." It was Mr. Otter; he popped his head up at the side of the boat.

Alice mumbled, "Sorry about that Mr. Otter." He looked at the boat and smiled.

He said, "It looks very good, may I have a go?"

"Yes," said *Alfie*.

Mr. Otter jumped on board and he turned the sail and off the boat went.

Alice and *Alfie* ran along the bank following him. By the time they reached the bridge they were worn out.

Mr. Otter floated underneath the bridge and called up to them, "I will be back soon."

All day they waited for him, but he never came back.

Alice said, "I hope he is alright, perhaps the bump on the head has something to do with not coming back."

200

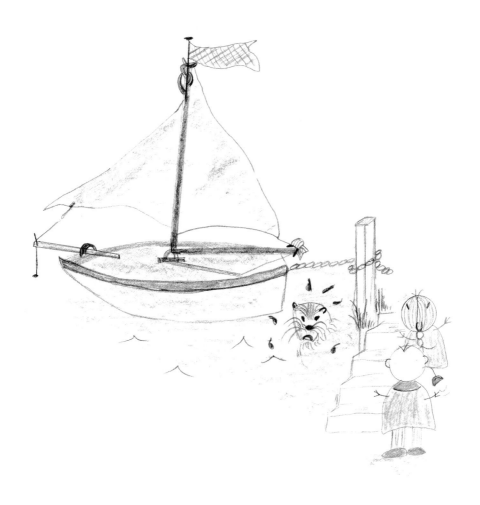

They decided to come back tomorrow to see if he had returned.

That night Mr. Moon said to *Alice* and *Alfie*, "Mr Otter's sail broke as he went over the weir, and the mast fell and hit him on the head again. He is o.k. as the swans are pulling him back. He should be home before daylight."

Alice and *Alfie* said goodnight to Mr. Moon and both dropped off to sleep, dreaming of the funny shaped pieces of wood in the barn.

When they woke up they both said at the same time, "It is a puzzle." They still did not know how it worked.

Later that morning Ted shouted up to *Alice* and *Alfie* in the windmill, "Look, look, Mr. Otter is back and he has two big humps on his head."

Ted went down to the boat and took over from Mr. Otter and he spent all day pretending he was a pirate, which pleased *Alice* and *Alfie* because he was not annoying them.

Jacques was in the kitchen baking cakes to take to his friend Kimmy.

Alice went out to the barn and the wooden pieces of the puzzle had all gone. She looked everywhere but could not find them.

Jacques had decided to go to town to do some shopping. As he walked past the barn to his old van Alice and Alfie saw he had a box in his hand with all the funny pieces of wood in it.

Alice and Alfie quickly jumped onto the back of the van and landed in the bucket.

Ted saw them, jumped off the boat and ran as fast as he could, but his little legs gave up and he shouted, "A pirates' life for me.

Jacques drove off down the lane with Alice and Alfie bouncing around in the bucket. When they arrived at the village, Jacques parked up outside the Art shop with lots of pictures hanging up in the window.

He grabbed the box with the funny wood and went Inside. As he opened the door an old bell rang, and the owner of the shop said, "Good morning, Jacques."

All Alice and Alfie could see were hand movements; then Jacques came back out of the shop without the box.

205

The man at the hardware shop said, "Good morning, Jacques. Please may I have some more bird boxes as I have sold out?"

"Certainly," Jacques replied.

As Jacques was walking down the road he met the lady from the fruit and veg shop. She asked him for more strawberries and more jars of honey. Jacques told them both that he would deliver everything in the morning.

All the way back home Jacques whistled an old French song. He was so happy with the order. He worked all afternoon.

The honey was easy as the bees had been working so hard, and Ted had kept his paws off the jars.

The next morning Jacques drove back to the village with his orders, and so did *Alice* and *Alfie*.

It was a lovely journey through the woods and along the side of the river.

Jacques delivered the strawberries and honey, then the bird boxes, and his pockets were full of money.

Just as he got back to his van, the lady from the Art shop shouted, "Jacques, I have finished!"

207

Jacques went back into the shop. *Alice* whispered to *Alfie*, "I wonder what she has finished?"

Jacques returned to the van carrying a small bag which was much smaller than the box that he had taken in the day before.

All the way back home *Alice* and *Alfie* tried to guess what was in the bag.

When they got back to the windmill Jacques went into the kitchen for his dinner.

Alice and *Alfie* went up the ladder and sat at the top of the stairs.

After dinner they heard Jacques snoring, so they crept downstairs and on the table was a book tied at the side with ribbon and, on the front, it said, "The Magic Windmill," different from all the other books they had seen.

Alice untied the ribbon and opened the book and inside were all the funny-shaped pieces of wood, all coloured, with parts of pictures on them. The cube with the numbers on was in the corner and under the pieces were a note. *Alice* said, "Ah, a book box."

It read:

'THE MAGIC WINDMILL PUZZLE
RULES OF THE GAME'

Alice and *Alfie* could not understand the Rules, but still decided to play their own game, their own rules.

Jacques started to stir from his sleep.

Alice quickly put the lid down on the book box, but she left the Rules and the dice on the table.

Jacques decided to go and work in the barn. He noticed the book box had been opened but could not work out how.

He saw *Alice* and *Alfie* in their bed box. "No, it could not have been them," he muttered to himself.

Just as Jacques left the kitchen, Ted had arrived back and was at the top of the stairs. He tripped and fell all the way down shouting, "Ouch, ouch."

As Jacques turned around Ted fell on the last step. Jacques muttered to himself, "The magic windmill keeps moving things around, I don't believe it."

That night *Alice*, *Alfie* and Ted played the jigsaw puzzle game instead of watching T.V.

Alice and *Alfie* loved all the pictures that the Art lady had drawn. They were beautiful.

There were different pictures of the windmill, the magic garden and the Wooden Prince at his Castle that *Alice* and *Alfie* had seen on their adventures.

They all played the game, and yes, I bet you can guess who won the game. You are right, it was Ted.

They put the book box game onto the shelf above the fireplace, and from then on, *Alice*, *Alfie* and Ted played the game every night.

The Moon told them, "I like the book box idea; perhaps Jacques should make them to sell as well, and I do like the picture of me on the front – he has definitely captured my good side."

213

"*Alice*, Ted is a wicked puzzle kid."

Alice and *Alfie*

A CHRISTMAS DREAM COMES TRUE

Jacques had decided to make more windmill puzzle games and sell them with the bird boxes at the Christmas Fair.

The puzzle that he made first was left in the kitchen and *Alice* and *Alfie* played most evenings.

A year had gone so quick and Christmas had arrived once again.

Alice said to *Alfie*, "We must make a special Christmas card for Nichole." This time she had come up with a plan. "We will slip it inside with Jacques' card for Nichole, so this time we know it will get there."

Alice found some white card and *Alfie* had found Jacques' old Christmas cards from last year. They cut up all the different pictures and stuck them to Nichole's card. It looked so magical, and of course it was one of a kind.

Alice and *Alfie* signed the card and Ted put his paw print down. They popped the card in the envelope, ready to be sent.

Every day they watched to see if Jacques had written his Christmas cards, ready to put their plan into action.

One very cold frosty morning *Alice* and *Alfie* came downstairs to sit next to the roaring log fire.

Jacques was outside clearing the frost off his van, while *Alice* had found his Christmas cards on the kitchen table and there, on the top, was Nichole's

Alice quickly switched the kettle on ready for Ted's old trick, steaming the envelope open. She slipped their Christmas card in with Jacques' and resealed it, just before Jacques came back into the kitchen.

He was whistling away and seemed to be happy that Christmas was here again.

The next day *Alice* and *Alfie* were woken up by the sound of Jacques' old van.

Alice ran to the window and shouted to *Alfie*, "Look, Jacques is putting two suitcases into the van. He must be going away for Christmas. Perhaps Nichole is coming to stay?"

Alfie whispered, "Perhaps, but don't get your hopes up, *Alice.*"

Ted woke up and said, "What is all the noise about?"

Alice told him, "It is nearly Christmas and Jacques has gone away."

Ted muttered, "Perhaps it will be a bit quieter around here!"

Just after Jacques had left, the postman arrived. He posted two letters through the box and they landed on the mat. *Alice* rushed over and picked them up. One was a bill and one was from England.

"Yes," she shouted, "It must be from Nichole."

She switched the kettle on and once again performed Ted's magic trick.

It read, "Sorry Jacques, the skiing trip if off as Tom has caught chicken pox."

Alfie asked, "What on earth is chicken pox?"

Ted replied, "Perhaps she has been laying eggs."

Alice just laughed.

Alice kept reading the letter and she told *Alfie*, "Nichole is saying they will come over in the New Year and perhaps stay longer."

221

Alice started to cry.

Ted ducked down in the bed box and muttered to himself, "Oh no, she is off again."

Alfie went over and gave *Alice* a cuddle, "Come on, at least you know Nichole is coming back in the New Year."

Alice and *Alfie* decided to go for a walk. It was a very crisp winter's morning with a bright blue sky, with one fluffy cloud and the Moon peeking just over the top.

Alice and *Alfie* waved at him as he slowly disappeared behind the cloud.

Alfie said, "He has gone to have a nap."

They walked towards the village and on the notice board on the green there was a large poster. It read:

'PANTOMIME THIS
CHRISTMAS EVE!'

The pantomime was Goldilocks and the Three Bears. *Alfie* chuckled and said to *Alice*, "We could change that to four bears, if we took Ted with us."

At the bottom of the poster it said,

'CHILDREN WITH TOYS, ESPECIALLY
BEARS, CAN COME IN FREE!'

Alice said, "Great, we can all get in for free. We will take Ted with us and it could be his Christmas present from us."

All the way back to the magic windmill *Alice* kept asking, "Who is Goldilocks?"

Alfie replied, "Perhaps it is a big grizzly bear!"

When they arrived at the windmill they told Ted about the pantomime and *Alice* told him they would pay.

Alfie winked at *Alice*.

Ted said, "Thank you, that is very kind of you both!"

Alfie told Ted, "I think there is going to be a big grizzly bear called Goldilocks."

Ted had bad dreams for the next week.

The day had arrived, and it was Christmas Eve and the whole village was going to the Pantomime.

GOLDILOCKS &
THE THREE BEARS

225

Alice and *Alfie* got dressed up; even Ted had brushed his fur.

When they arrived in the village there was a long queue of families waiting to go into the hall.

Alfie said, "Look, there is a sign saying, 'Stage Door, actors only.' Come on, Ted is always acting."

The side door was slightly open and they all went in. They could hear all the families in the hall and up at the front was the stage, but nobody around.

Ted whispered, "I have always wanted to be in a show!"

Ted gently opened the curtain and quickly shut it. There were hundreds of children in front of the stage, sitting on chairs.

Alice said, "Come on, we must go around to the side of the stage."

As they walked across the stage they did not see the net on the floor. *Alice* and *Alfie* stepped onto it, Ted walked into a rope hanging from above. He grabbed hold of it and as he pulled the net went flying up in the air with *Alice* and *Alfie* inside it.

227

Suddenly the stage curtains opened and the parents and the children all started laughing.

Ted was swinging around on the rope and *Alice* and *Alfie* were doing the same in the net ten feet up.

The Compere walked onto the stage and said to everybody, "We hope you will like the show tonight." He could not understand why everybody was laughing and as he looked around he thought, "This trio are not in the show!"

He grabbed Ted and the net fell onto the floor.

He picked up *Alice* and *Alfie*, turned and apologised to the crowd, "Sorry about that. One of the teddy bears has escaped!"

He put *Alice* and *Alfie* on a ledge at the side of the stage. There they would be able to see the whole show. The Compere told everyone there would be a change of plan and they now had four bears in the show.

He said, "But thank goodness, only one Goldilocks."

The curtain shut and then there was silence. They were all waiting for the show to begin.

229

As the curtain went back, Goldilocks walked on stage and everybody applauded. She was beautiful, with long blonde hair, and in her hand she was carrying Ted.

Ted's dream had come true! He was in the show! The other three bears were not very happy that Ted had stolen the show.

Alice and *Alfie* had the best view. After the show had finished and everyone had gone home, Goldilocks came over to *Alice* and *Alfie* and asked them, "Now who do you belong to?"

She picked them up and noticed the little tags which read, "*Alice* and *Alfie* and the magic windmill."

Ted's tags said, "Made in England!"

She told them, "It is your lucky day, your home is on my way."

As Goldilocks walked out of the stage door, holding *Alice*, *Alfie* and Ted, the church bells struck midnight. She said, "We must be on our way."

Suddenly there was a flash of colour flying through the sky and a faint outline of reindeer and a loud cry. "Ho, ho, ho and off we go."

231

Alfie said, "Father Christmas is back again."

Goldilocks jumped onto her scooter and off she sped.

Alice, *Alfie* and Ted had never been on a scooter before, whizzing along with their hair flapping in the wind.

When they arrived at the windmill Goldilocks knocked on the door, but there was no answer.

The Moon floated down and just as Goldilocks looked up she dropped Ted. He quickly grabbed the door handle and it opened.

Goldilocks put *Alice* and *Alfie* to bed but did not know what to do with Ted, so she sat him in the rocking chair. She said, "Goodnight," and went on her way.

The next morning *Alfie* shouted up to *Alice*, "He's been."

Alice ran downstairs and there were presents on the table.

Alfie said, "Oh no, we forgot about the Tree!"

233

They all opened their presents, and all had new scarves and diaries.

In the front of *Alice's* diary it read, 'Together for good, Love Nichole.'

Alice asked *Alfie*, "What does that mean?"

His and Ted's diaries both read the same.

Alice said, "This has been the best Christmas ever but if only our Christmas wish would come true."

That night the Moon shone down and told them, "Nichole sends her love and your Christmas wish will come true."

235

"Alfie, You are right, Ted is a real Actor!"

Alice and *Alfie*

HAPPY NEW YEAR

237

It was boxing day and *Alice*, *Alfie* and Ted decided to go out for a walk.

Little did they know that it had been snowing all night.

Alfie opened the back door and to his amazement a wall of white snow was in front of him. He kicked, it, but it did not move.

He shouted to *Alice*, "Come and have a look at this."

Ted was on the rocking chair and blurted out, "That means only one thing."

Alice and *Alfie* looked at him, "Go on," said *Alice*.

Ted had a grin on his face then he cried out, "Drip, he must be back.

Alice said, "I think you mean Mr. Snowman?"

"Yes, Drip," he replied.

They all ran upstairs and looked out of the bedroom window. The snow was not as deep as they thought. It had blown up into the back door porch. They saw ski prints down in the yard.

Alice said, "There must be someone here."

Alice and *Alfie* put on their coats and scarves and tied their boots and slid down the ladder.

Ted shouted out, "I'm staying indoors! It is too cold for me."

Alice and *Alfie* followed the ski prints. They went out of the yard and down the lane.

Alfie said, "I am going back to the barn to get our skis." He returned five minutes later and off they went.

The snow was still falling, and they had to keep wiping their faces.

Alfie said, "I wonder who is on the skis?"

As they came down towards the church the ski prints stopped at the post box outside the vicarage.

Alice opened the post box and there inside was a small scroll. It was wrapped in crepe paper with a ribbon tied round and a wax stamp.

Alice opened the scroll and read what it said to *Alfie*.

POSTES

241

You are invited to the bash of the year
It's at the magic castle don't fear
Bring your partner and good cheer
To welcome in the New Year
You must come in fancy dress
And not in a vest
Remember it's a winter wonderland
And we have a wonderful band
Food for all
It's going to be a ball

From the Wooden Prince

R.S.V.P.

Alice said to *Alfie*, "It does not have a name on it so we could take it and go."

Alfie said, "No, no, no…yes!"

Alice said, "Make your mind up."

Alfie said, "When I said no, I meant yes."

242

243

Alice whispered, "Quick, we must go – the vicar is coming out of the church."

They hid behind the wall and the vicar came across and opened the post box and looked inside. He muttered to himself, "I though I saw someone put a letter in."

Alfie whispered to *Alice*, "No, no, no, yes."

"Ssssh," she replied. "Have you hit your head, because what you are saying does not make sense?"

The vicar went back into the church and *Alice* and *Alfie* went off on their skis, back to the magic windmill.

Ted had cleared all the snow away from the back door. He had been very clever; he had plugged the hair dryer in and melted all the snow.

Alfie said, "Very good Ted, you have used your brain for once."

Alice said, "Look on the door." There was a bag tied to the knocker. She took it down and opened it. Inside was another scroll, just like the one they had taken from the vicarage.

244

Alice said to *Alfie*, "You are going to have to take the scroll back to the vicarage."

He shouted, "No, no, no," and before he could take another breath *Alice* stamped her feet and shouted, "Yes."

All the way he muttered to himself, "I'm the Drip, not Mr. Snowman."

When he eventually arrived back at the magic windmill he was like an icicle, so *Alice* put him in front of the log fire to warm him up.

Alice had been thinking what they could wear to the grand ball. Something long and tall.

Ted said, "What about a scarecrow?

Alfie laughed and cried, "You do know you are not invited, Ted, your name is not on the invitation."

Ted replied, "I did not want to go anyway. I would rather be on my own on New Year's Eve, at least I won't have to kiss anyone!"

247

Over the next couple of days *Alice* and *Alfie* were thinking what they could dress as. Then *Alice* decided, SNOWMEN.

Ted said, "What, two more Drips? That is all we need."

So *Alice* sewed up two old sheets with buttons on the front and two for the eyes. She made two orange noses out of card.

Alfie put his on first; he looked amazing. *Alice* tried hers on just as Ted was coming down the stairs.

Alice asked Ted, "Can you recognise us?"

"Yes, you are *Alice* and *Alfie*, your tags are sticking out of the back."

Alice folded up the snowman outfits and put them in a safe place.

New Year's Eve arrived. *Alice* said, "I cannot wait for tonight. It is going to be a ball."

Alice shouted upstairs to Ted, "Come down. I would like to have a word with you. Tonight is for celebrating so you must come with us. I have made you a fancy-dress costume. Now shut your eyes."

Alice put a white cloth over him, rolled him over and zipped up the back.

She said, "Now open your eyes."

Ted shouted out, "What am I?"

Alice said, "Well what comes before a drip?"

He looked up in the air and said, "I don't know."

Alice told him, "A snowball."

Ted rolled round and round the kitchen knocking into everything.

Alice shouted, "Wait one moment, stop." She cut two eyes out of the cloth and then Ted could see. He just loved it.

The time had come to go to the ball. As they walked out of the magic windmill door, a horse and sleigh had just drawn up into the courtyard. *Alice* shut the door, while *Alfie* said, "I will hold Ted, sorry I mean snowball."

On the sleigh were the vicar and his wife and children.

The man at the front of the sleigh whispered to *Alice* and *Alfie*, "Quick, jump on the back." And off they went to the magic castle.

The vicar was dressed as an elf and his wife was a cat, and their children were mice, all looking very nice.

After a long drive they all arrived at the magic castle.

It was all lit up like a palace in a fairy tale.

They all walked up to the front door while the vicar rang the bell. The doors opened and there was Father Christmas.

Alfie went up to him and whispered, "You are working late!"

Father Christmas replied, "Yes, overtime, but I don't mind."

They all walked in, apart from Ted. He was in *Alfie's* hand. The place was so magical. There were trumpets blowing, and lace hanging from the ceiling which looked like icicles. The lights were all the colours of the rainbow. At the end of the great hall there was a table full of food.

253

The room was full of Kings and Queens, and others dressed from beautiful themes.

The Wooden Prince took pride of place sitting on the mantel piece. He shouted out, "This year has not been grate!" Everybody laughed. "This New Year will give everybody good cheer."

As the clock struck midnight the bells and trumpeters welcomed in the New Year. Then from the ceiling above, balloons dropped and popped. There was a wish in every balloon.

Alice and *Alfie* grabbed a wish and it read, "Don't forget, only wish upon a star."

Ted tried to catch a wish but was beaten by one of the mice, who showed him the door. He went rolling out down the draw bridge and landed in a heap of snow.

Alice and *Alfie* went running out to find him. They heard his little voice but could not see him.

Alice said, "Look there are two little eyes peeking out of that snow drift."

Alfie went and picked him up and brushed him off.

They all went back into the castle to join the party.

Alice and *Alfie* danced all night while Ted rolled and rolled until he hit the table with a loud bang.

As he unzipped his costume, there in front of him was his biggest wish, a table full of his favourite food and a large jar of honey. He grabbed it and hid under the table.

Alice said to *Alfie*, "I think it is time we should go and say goodnight to the Wooden Prince."

The Prince said, "I have made you all up a doggie bag as there is so much food left."

Ted said, "The party has been great, and good night old mate!"

As they walked back to the magic windmill others walked past, thinking they were real snowmen.

As they arrived home they heard a voice shout out, "Good night, old drips." As they looked around It was Mr. Snowman, having the last laugh.

That night the Moon wished them all a Happy New Year. And Nichole's star twinkled with a tear.

257

Alfie, "Thank you for being my best friend."

Alice and *Alfie*

A STORY NEVER TO BE TOLD

It was New Year's Day and *Alice* and *Alfie* had wished each other a very Happy New Year.

Ted just mumbled as he walked out of the bedroom. He tripped up on the old rug on the landing. He tumbled over and hit his head on the door, and shouted, "That's a good start to the New Year." Ted stood up with a lovely new bump on his head.

Ted went off in a huff, not even telling *Alice* and *Alfie* where he was going.

Alice was going to put the rug straight when she saw one of the floorboards was loose. She put her foot on one end and the board flew up into the air.

Alfie said, "It has never done that before."

Alice replied, "Because the rug has always covered it."

There under the floor was a bright red and gold leather bound book.

Alice picked it up and went and sat on the bed.

Alfie asked, "What is it about?"

260

Alice said, "Let us see."

On the front was the word in gold lettering, but it was all in French. She had kept Jacques' French to English dictionary.

Alice started to cry.

Alfie asked, "Why are you crying?"

Alice replied, "Well the dictionary always reminds me of Nichole."

Alfie whispered, "Don't worry, she will be back soon; it is written in the stars."

Alice opened the dictionary and after a while she had worked out what the book was called.

Alfie said, "Come on, I'm waiting."

Alice said, "It's called, 'A Story Never to Be Told.'"

Alfie scratched his head and said, "I don't understand. If it is a story, it must be told."

"Yes, you are right," *Alice* replied.

She opened the book up. It was beautiful. Sketches on every page, all hand drawn, with writing under every picture.

It was all about the magic windmill, over one hundred years ago. In the front of the book was a note and it had a signature on it. *Alice* spent two hours translating from French to English. It read:

The magic windmill
is the place to be
making your thoughts run free
I have written and drawn this book
so, whoever you are can have a look.
Once you have read the book
put it back in the nook
It is a story never to be told
keep it as memories till your old

signed Chantelle 1908
somewhere in heaven

265

Alice said to *Alfie*, "There are too many words in French to translate, so let us look at the pictures and try to work out what the story is about."

The book was amazing, all about Chantelle. She had a magical childhood at the windmill with her parents.

Every one of her pictures told her story. She used to pick the fruit and veg in the magic garden and her best friends were the Moon and the stars.

It was as if *Alice* and *Alfie* were walking in her footsteps.

They were only half way through the book when the night sky covered the windmill.

Ted had arrived back at the windmill. He struggled climbing the ladder but finally fell into the bedroom window.

He had honey all round his mouth and over his paws and a bump he got from the door in the morning.

He was in a right old state and decided to go to bed.

Alice and *Alfie* sat on the window sill looking at the book.

The Moon shone down and said to *Alice* and *Alfie*,
"I have seen that book before. It was a long time ago
and the title was 'A Story Never to Be Told.' A little girl
called Chantelle wrote it for memories only."

The Moon told them to close their eyes and he would
take them on a journey back in time.

He asked them where they would like to go. *Alice*
told him that she would like to go back to 1908 to meet
Chantelle.

Mr. Moon told her, "Your wish will come true. Now let
me try to remember the spell. Six times around Nichole's
star… now open your eyes and see where you are."

Alice and *Alfie* were still at the magic windmill, still
sitting on the window sill, but the place looked so
different; down in the yard were lots of horses and carts.
The fields were full of corn and wheat and the windmill
was working so hard.

They heard a voice and *Alice* and *Alfie* turned around
and there, sitting on the bed, was a little girl. She asked,
"Who are you?"

Alice told her their names.

269

The little girl said, "My name is Chantelle."

Alice said, "I can guess you are eight years of age and writing your book."

Chantelle had colouring pens in her hand and said, "Yes, how did you know?"

Alice told her, "We have seen your book in the future."

The little girl asked the rag dolls, "What is the future?"

Alfie said, "It is a long time away."

Chantelle told them, "I have nearly finished my book about my time at the magic windmill, but I have no title for it."

Alice grinned, "Yes you have, it is called 'A Story Never to be Told.'

Chantelle said, "I like that."

Alice and *Alfie* sat and helped her finish the book.

The little girl told them she must hide it in a very special place.

271

Alfie said to Chantelle, "What about under the floorboard on the landing?"

It was the same rug lying on the floor. *Alfie* lifted the rug and there was the loose floorboard.

Alice took the book from Chantelle and put it under the floor.

The little girl said, "Goodbye, and remember, "A Story Never to be Told."

Alfie put the floorboard back and put the rug back down.

As they turned around Chantelle had vanished. They ran to the window and as they looked out everything had gone forward to present time.

That night the Moon shone down and whispered to *Alice* and *Alfie*, Remember,

"A Story Never to be Told"

273

"*Alice*, our future is safe in this beautiful place."

Alice and *Alfie*

THE PRAM RACE

Christmas was well in the past and *Alice* and *Alfie* could not wait for the Spring and Summer to arrive.

Early one morning the letterbox opened, and *Alice* went and picked up all the letters off the mat. All there was were bills and one leaflet. It read:

'FOR THE FIRST TIME
THE GREAT VILLAGE PRAM RACE
WITH A TWIST

ADULTS ONLY
NO BABIES

AND ALL IN FANCY DRESS
SUNDAY MORNING
AT THE VILLAGE GREEN

A SILVER CUP FOR THE WINNER
AND
A DUMMY FOR THE LOSERS'

Alfie looked at *Alice* and said, "Are you thinking what I am thinking?"

Alice replied, "Yes, out in the old barn is the old French pram. What are we going to dress up in and which one of us is going to be the baby in the pram?"

Just at that moment Ted walked down the stairs.

Alfie looked straight at Ted and said, "That's one problem out the way!"

Ted shrugged his shoulders and replied, "I'm not a problem, am I?"

Alice and *Alfie* sat Ted down and told him about the Pram Race. Then they dressed him up like a baby; he looked brilliant.

Alice and *Alfie* decided to go out into the barn to check out the old French pram.

As they slid down the ladder *Alice* shouted, "Hello." The bird box had different sorts of birds to last year.

Alfie shouted, "Must go, have a good moving-in day, see you later."

In the barn over in the corner was an old sheet that was covering lots of old junk. They slipped the sheet off and underneath there were lots of boxes and buckets and there was the old French pram. They pulled it out and spent all morning cleaning it. "It's perfect," said *Alice*. "Now what are we going to dress up as? We cannot be rag dolls."

Alice and *Alfie* went over and sat on the straw bales.

Suddenly a voice shouted out, "Ouch, ouch. Is it time to go out into the field?" It was Mr. Scarecrow.

Alfie said, "We are so sorry, we did not see you lying on the straw bales as you look just like one."

Mr. Scarecrow walked over to the barn door and looked up at the sun.

"No, it is one month too early for me to go out into the field," he replied.

Alice said, "We are really sorry to have woken you up."

Mr. Scarecrow looked at the old French pram and said, "What is going on?"

Alice told him, "On Sunday morning there is a pram race down on the village green. *Alfie* and I don't know what to dress as. Ted is the baby."

Mr. Scarecrow suggested, "You could dress up as scarecrows as there is lots of straw here in the barn. All you would need is jackets, trousers, old hats and lots of string."

280

281

Mr. Scarecrow told them to come back early Sunday morning before the race and he would help them dress up.

Alice and *Alfie* went back indoors just as Jacques had arrived home. The telephone had rung, and he was talking to Mr. Rag and said, "See you in the village in the morning."

Alice looked at *Alfie* and she said, "Brilliant, all our problems solved. Mr. Rag will have all the jackets, trousers and hats that we need."

The next morning, they woke early and went out to the old van and jumped into the bucket and waited for Jacques. Eventually, he came out of the windmill and went over to the barn, picked up the old boxes full of junk and put them in the van. Then he went back into the barn and came back with the old French pram.

Alice looked at *Alfie* and said, "No, no, no, the pram is for us on Sunday, so we can win the silver cup. We will have to do something."

When they arrived at the village Mr. Rag was waiting in the car park and he walked over to Jacques' van.

Mr. Rag said to Jacques, "I would love to buy your old French pram, but first we must have breakfast."

Alice and *Alfie* jumped out of the bucket and *Alfie* pulled the pram off the back of the van with a big bump.

Ted shouted, "Ouch." Then Ted's face popped up out of the pram.

Alfie said, "What are you doing in there?"

Ted explained, "I am just trying the pram out for Sunday's big race. I am the baby, you know."

Alice asked, "Now what are we going to do with the pram?"

They looked around as the church bells started ringing.

Alice said, "The church, let us hide it in there and we can come back for it before Sunday morning service."

"Brilliant," *Alfie* replied.

Alice opened the church door and had a quick look inside. The people were two bell ringers practising up in the tower. They pushed the pram into the church at the back of the pews and covered it over with a sheet that Jacques had left in the pram.

Alice, Alfie and Ted went back outside and saw Jacques and Mr. Rag coming back to the van.

When they looked inside the van they saw that the old French pram had disappeared.

They both scratched their heads and looked around, but no pram to be seen.

Alice and *Alfie* decided to walk back to the magic windmill. They went into the barn and told Mr. Scarecrow what had happened.

He laughed then asked, "Where is baby Ted?"

Alfie said, "Oh no, he is still in the pram in the church."

Alice and *Alfie* walked all the way back to the church. When they arrived, the bells had stopped ringing and the church door was locked with a note on it saying, 'Closed until Sunday 8.00 a.m.'

Alice and *Alfie* shouted, "Ted are you alright?" But there was no reply.

Ted was fast asleep inside the pram.

287

Alice and *Alfie* had no choice but to leave him and come back as planned on Sunday at 8 a.m. with food and drink for him.

Alfie said, "He is going to be a very unhappy baby Ted."

Alice replied, "You mean he will be his old self then?"

"Yes," *Alfie* replied.

As they walked across the village green they saw lots of people queuing at the village hall.

There was a sign saying, 'Mr. Rag's Jumble Sale. Doors open mid-day.'

They did not have to wait long. As Mr. Rag started to ring the bell all the people came rushing in, tripping over *Alice* and *Alfie*.

They picked themselves up and walked into the hall.

Alfie said, "Look, clothes and hats for Sunday's race!" But every time *Alice* picked up a hat somebody snatched it from her.

She said to *Alfie*, "That's not fair."

Alfie had been clever; he had dragged a pile of hats and clothes down under the table and he had grabbed a lovely old leather case. He grabbed *Alice's* leg and quickly pulled her down under the table.

"Look, I have got everything we need," *Alfie* shouted.

The only problem they had was Mr. Rag, who was at the front door taking the money.

Alice said, "We must distract him, somehow."

Alfie saw an umbrella in the corner next to the door. He went over and opened it right in front of Mr. Rag.

He shouted to *Alice*, "Quick, run around the back of Mr. Rag."

"O.k." whispered *Alice*.

Mr. Rag was startled by the umbrella.

He shouted, "That is bad luck, putting an umbrella up indoors," and grabbed hold of the handle.

Alfie quickly slipped between his legs and the job was done.

Alfie met *Alice* outside and walked back to the magic windmill, taking turns in carrying the suitcase.

When they arrived home, they went into the barn and showed Mr. Scarecrow what they had found at the jumble sale.

He told them that they had everything, even the straw, but one thing that was missing was the baby.

Alice told him what had happened and Mr. Scarecrow laughed.

On Saturday night *Alice* and *Alfie* asked Mr. Moon to grant them a wish to win the race.

He said, "Just do your best and have fun, and bring the cup back when you have won."

Alice said to him, "Do you think we are going to win?"

He just had a grin!

Alice and *Alfie* woke early on Sunday morning and ran out to the barn.

Mr. Scarecrow was still fast asleep, dreaming of scaring pigeons out in the field.

Alfie shook Mr. Scarecrow who sat up, still dreaming, going, "Coo, coo."

Alice said, "It is time to get us dressed."

Mr. Scarecrow helped by stuffing the clothes with the straw, then laid some across the top of their heads, and on went their hats.

Mr. Scarecrow smiled and said, "You look just like me."

Alice and *Alfie* walked to the village and when they reached the church the door was slightly open.

They had Ted's baby clothes with them; now all they had to do was find baby!

They crept into the church and lifted the sheet off the pram, but to their surprise no Ted, he had gone!

As they stood there, the vicar walked in with Ted in his arms.

Alice and *Alfie* dropped to the floor and fortunately the vicar did not see them.

The vicar put Ted in the pram and left it in front of the altar.

Alice and *Alfie* quickly jumped up, grabbed the pram and out the door they ran.

They dressed Ted as the baby and Ted told *Alice* and *Alfie* what a lovely time he had had at the vicarage. Honey and cakes with children singing songs.

Alice said, "Typical, we were worried about you and all the time you were having fun."

It was midday and the church bells started to ring and the prams started to arrive.

There were clowns, sailors, tramps, and of course scarecrows, *Alice* and *Alfie*.

They were all given maps with clues.

Alice and *Alfie* knew all the answers before the race had started.

The hooter rang and off they all went, writing the answers to the clues as they ran.

The clowns had no idea and stopped so many times. The tramps kept losing their trousers and the sailors totally ship-wrecked!

297

Alice and *Alfie* were way ahead; they had been to the railway station and found the answer, the 10.45 to La Rochelle.

The next question was, 'Who is the owner of the magic windmill?' Easy, *Alfie* wrote 'Jacques.'

Question number four, 'What was the Prince from the castle made of?' *Alice* scribbled, "Wood of course."

When they reached the bakery they were asked, 'How many pies in a baker's dozen?'

Alfie shouted, "Thirteen."

They carried on answering all the clues until the last one, 'Who was in the picnic?'

Ted winked and replied, "Me, of course."

They arrived back at the village green and were twenty minutes ahead of all the others.

At the presentation *Alice*, *Alfie* and Ted won the lovely Silver Cup and the clowns were the losers who looked funny with the dummies in the mouths.

Alice, *Alfie* and Ted were applauded for winning the pram race and left with smiles on their faces.

299

Alice and *Alfie* pushed the pram all the way back to the magic windmill.

Jacques had an idea what was going on and he had made a space on the mantle of the fire place for the special cup, where it took pride of place.

Alice, *Alfie* and Ted went out to the barn and thanked Mr. Scarecrow for his help just before he was due to start his new season in the field.

Alice and *Alfie* sat at the bedroom window and Mr. Moon floated down and congratulated them on winning the pram race.

Just before he wished them good night, he whispered, "Your dream is about to come true."

Alice and *Alfie* asked, "Mr. Moon, what do you mean?"

He just smiled and drifted away!

"*Alfie*, What does Mr. Moon know that we don't?"

Alice and *Alfie*

A MAGIC ENDING

Alice and *Alfie* were exhausted from the pram race. Pushing Ted was something they would not normally do as he was as fit as a fiddle. So why was he the one in the rocking chair fast asleep?

The silver cup looked magnificent on the mantel piece next to the other cups they had won.

The Summer had arrived and the flowers were out in full bloom. The magic garden was full of fruit and veg and all the animals were so happy.

There was cricket every day and Colin the mole had been made umpire. He could come up at a minute's notice.

Mr. and Mrs. Owl were now the proud parents of a fluffy white owl which *Alfie* had named 'Chirpy,' as that was all the noise it made.

Jacques had gone into town early and when he arrived back, his van was full of wooden tea chests.

Alice said to *Alfie*, "What is he going to do with all of those?"

Alfie replied, "Perhaps his going to make tea!"

Alice added, "He cannot make tea; the leaves come from Asia."

Ted walked into the kitchen and asked, "Is Jacques moving?"

Alice asked him what he meant.

"I have seen packing cases like that before, when I lived with Cleo in England. Her neighbours moved and that is what they used." *Alice* started to cry.

Alfie told her, "No, that cannot be, Jacques is part of the furniture, just like us."

Later that morning Jacques came into the windmill for lunch. As he sat in his rocking chair the phone rang. *Alice* and *Alfie* sat at the top of the stairs and listened.

Jacques was speaking to somebody called Marcell and said, "I definitely want to now and will see you tomorrow with all the paperwork."

Jacques went back outside while *Alice* and *Alfie* watched him walk towards the barn. He turned and glanced at the magic windmill. They saw Jacques wipe tears from his eyes; then he disappeared into the barn. All day and night they were worried as they did not know what was going on.

The next morning the sun was high in the sky, shining a beautiful light over the windmill.

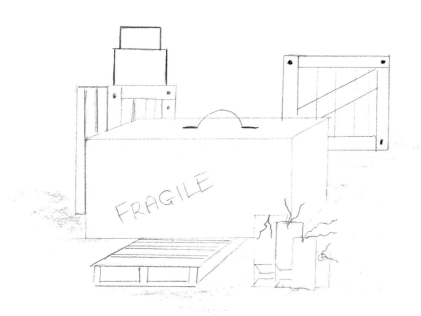

307

Later that morning *Alice* heard a vehicle drive into the yard. She looked out of the window and saw Jacques in the yard talking to a man, "Bonjour, Marcell, let us go in and have a coffee and sign the paperwork."

Alice said to *Alfie*, "What paperwork, what is Jacques up to?"

After a while Marcell left and Jacques returned to the barn.

Alice and *Alfie* decided to walk to the park to play on the swings and slide.

As they were walking to the end of the drive they could see Marcell and his van at the main gate. He was hammering a large pole into the ground. Then he fitted a board with writing on it. As he drove away *Alice* and *Alfie* went to have a look. The sign was written in French.

Just at that moment Mr. Owl came flying down and landed on the sign. "Jacques has put the windmill up for sale then?"

Alice could not stop crying so *Alfie* suggested they go to the bakery to get one of her favourite cakes to cheer her up. It was their lucky day - a tray of croissants had just been delivered, and they grabbed one each and walked along the street.

The office at the end of the village was very busy and in the window were pictures of houses.

Alice said, "Why would you want to buy a picture of a house?" In the middle of the window was a picture of the magic windmill.

Just then the baker walked past and said to his wife, "Look, Jacques has got the windmill up for sale. He must be moving."

Alice dropped her croissant and ran all the way to the park. She sat on the swing and *Alfie* came to push her. Once again, she was crying. "What is going to happen to us when Jacques moves?"

Alfie said, "We can all stay. It is our home and we could live in the magic garden with the animals."

Alice and *Alfie* walked back to the windmill.

Jacques was in the kitchen packing and cleaning. He was whistling a French song.

Alice asked *Alfie*, "How could he be so happy when he is leaving the windmill behind?" *Alice* was so tired of thinking, she climbed into the bed box.

311

Suddenly she found the Christmas card from Nichole. She opened it up and there inside was a pressed rose. It looked amazing. She showed *Alfie* then went off to sleep.

Alfie took the card and went out into the barn. He had a brainwave, "I know what will cheer *Alice* up." He decided to make a magic windmill flower press.

Jacques had left all his tools on the bench and plenty of wood. *Alfie* cut and drilled and in no time, he had made the little flower press for *Alice*. He painted it and drew the sails on. Then he drew a picture of him and *Alice* at the window and went back to the windmill.

As *Alfie* was climbing the ladder, Mr. Moon shone down and told him and *Alice* not to worry, as it would all come out in the wash. As Mr. Moon floated away *Alfie* shouted, "What wash?" But by this time Mr. Moon was too far away.

Alfie climbed in through the window and woke *Alice*. He said, "Look what I have made to cheer you up."

Alfie took the flower press from behind his back.

Alice asked, "What is it?" Alfie showed her how it worked and said, "There is a special flower already in it."

Alice said, "Thank you, Alfie, you are my best friend."

Ted walked in and asked, "What about me?"

Alice replied, "Yes, you are our best friend too."

The next morning there was a commotion in the yard. When they looked out of the window they saw a family with their dog. Marcell the Agent was showing them around the windmill as Jacques had gone out, because he could not bear to be around.

The family had a good look at the windmill. The rag dolls were picked up, then put down by the children. The Mum said, "It is too small, very dull and not for us." Alice gave a sigh of relief.

Day after day the same thing was said. Then one afternoon, when Alice and Alfie were collecting flowers for the flower press, they saw Marcell at the top of the lane changing the board.

Once again Mr. Owl told them, "Hey, that was quick, Jacques has sold the windmill."

MOULIN
à vent
vendu
.0263 4921

315

Alice could not hold back the tears. Who had brought the place, could they stay, or would they have to leave?

Alfie said, "We could always go and live at the magic castle - we have the key to the door and we could always come back to visit."

Alice just cried more. She dropped the flower basket and ran back to the magic windmill.

Alfie picked up the flowers and followed her back, wondering how this would end up.

Jacques spent the next two weeks packing. The tea chests were all filled and ready to go.

One morning the rag dolls heard Jacques talking to Marcell on the phone. "Yes, Friday 13th August is fine for me to move out."

Alfie said to *Alice*, "That is at the end of the week."

Every night the Moon shone down and told *Alice* and *Alfie* that it was going to be a magic ending.

Friday morning arrived *Alice* and *Alfie* watched the removal lorry loading all of Jacques' furniture.

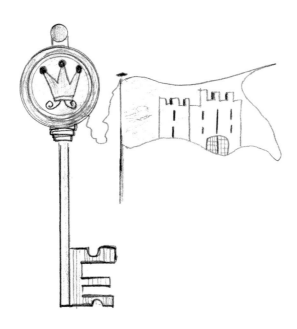

Alice and *Alfie* could not watch any longer and decided to go for a very long walk.

All their friends kept saying, "Don't worry." Mr. and Mrs. Owl said, "Look on the bright side, the place would be cleaned from top to bottom."

Alice replied, "Yes, but what if the new owners do not want us?"

Mr. Owl replied, "Magic is on your side!"

Colin the mole popped up and said, "I have heard it is going to be a very special day."

Even the seagulls told them it was going to be the most magical day they had ever had.

Alice and *Alfie* had been out all day and decided to go back to the windmill.

When they arrived home, they saw Ted messing around on the boat. *Alice* asked him, "Why are you so happy?"

"I have just found two jars of honey which I hid on the boat," he grinned.

When they arrived back at the magic windmill Jacques had gone and it was very earie, not a sound, just a note pinned to the door.

Sorry Alice, Alfie and Ted
I Looked everywhere for you
But don't worry you will all be fine.
I will miss you
Love Jacques xxx

Alice, Alfie and Ted climbed the ladder with tears in their eyes. They cuddled up and fell asleep. The Moon floated by with a big smile on his face.

They were woken by noises in the yard. They looked out of the window and there were two lorries with English number plates. Suddenly the door opened and Nichole shouted, "*Alice, Alfie*, we're home!"

"*Alfie*, now, that is what I call a magic ending!"

THE END

The magic windmill is a very special place
When Alice and Alfie arrived with their case.

Mr. Moon and Nichole's star
Have looked after them from afar

The Summers have been hot
The Winters cold
Secret stories never to be told

Even Ted they did dread
But now a special friend instead

The windmill's power
The scent of a flower

The journey has been long
But just like the song
Must come to an end

Now you have read the story
In all its glory

Now Jacques the keeper has gone
His memories will live on
From his bird box and honey and all the rest
Alice and Alfie thought he was the best

Now Au Revoir it's time for bed
Love Alice, Alfie and our friend Ted xxx

Loykey & Lillybit books

Alice and *Alfie* and the magic windmill

Alice and *Alfie* and the magic windmill
The Return of Nichole

Alice and *Alfie* and the magic windmill
Best Friends

******

The Shadow of Old London Town

www.loykeylillybit.co.uk

322